DOGS
AND
PUPPIES
IN CROSS-STITCH

DOGS AND PUPPIES

IN CROSS-STITCH

Charted Designs By

JULIE S. HASLER

BLANDFORD

Colour photography by
James Mayer of cross-stitch
embroidery by Joyce Freel

A BLANDFORD BOOK

First published in the UK 1989 by Blandford Press,
Villiers House, 41/47 Strand,
London, WC2N 5JE

Reprinted 1990

Copyright © 1989 Blandford Press

Distributed in the United States by
Sterling Publishing Co, Inc,
387 Park Avenue South, New York, NY 10016

Distributed in Australia by
Capricorn Link (Australia) Pty Ltd
PO Box 665, Lane Cove, NSW 2066

British Library Cataloguing in Publication Data
Hasler, Julie S.
  Dogs and puppies in cross-stitch: charted
  designs.
  1.   Embroidery. Cross-stitch – Patterns
  I.   Title
  746.44

    ISBN 0 7137 2006 9 (Paperback)
    ISBN 0 7137 2219 3 (Hardback)

Typeset by Inforum Ltd, Portsmouth
Printed in Great Britain by the Alden Press, Oxford

Contents

Preface   7

General Directions   9
Techniques   10
Cross-stitch   10
Backstitch   10
Materials   12
Preparing to Work   13
Finishing   14
The Charted Designs   15
The Breeds   17
Decorative Panels and Borders   67

Index of Breeds   79

Preface

The favourite stitch of our great-grandmothers, cross-stitch is becoming increasingly popular in these modern times for the decoration of household furnishings, linen, children's clothes, in fact anything which lends itself to this type of embroidery. The possibilities are endless.

Cross-stitch is one of the simplest, most versatile and elegant needlecrafts, and examples of its use can be found in many different countries and different eras.

The projects in this book make beautiful gifts for family and friends: gifts with a personal touch which have taken time and care to create, which will still be treasured long after shop-bought gifts have been forgotten.

The designs in this book can be worked by following the charts exactly, or, by using your imagination, you can create your own designs by the use of alternative colours or by combining different motifs from several charts to create embroideries which are uniquely yours.

General directions

The designs in this book are created for counted cross-stitch, a very enjoyable craft which you will find easy to learn and inexpensive as well!

The fabric you choose to sew your designs on and the number of strands of silk you use is your choice.

You will find that the fabric is available in varying thread counts, and that there is a very wide choice of colours: white, ecru, pink, blue, lemon and pale green, to name but a few.

I chose 11-count cotton aida in ecru to sew the designs in this book, using three strands of embroidery cotton for the cross-stitch. Why not use your imagination and choose a fabric colour that will enhance your embroidery?

The charts are easy to read. Each square on the chart represents one stitch to be taken on the fabric and each different symbol represents a different colour, the empty squares being background fabric.

A colour key is given with each design.

If you wish to decorate clothing with any of the designs in this book, the most satisfactory method is to work the design over cross-stitch fabric basted to the clothing material and remove the cross-stitch fabric afterwards, thread by thread. This will leave the cross-stitch embroidery on the clothing material beneath.

Relax, enjoy sewing the designs, and make something beautiful for you and your home.

Techniques

Cross-stitch

To begin: bring the thread through at the lower right-hand side, leaving a short length of thread on the underside of the work and anchoring it with the first few stitches as in Diagrams 1 and 2. Insert the needle across the mesh into the next hole above and diagonally to the left and bring it out through the hole across the mesh but immediately below. Half the stitch is now completed.

Continue in the same way to the end of the row. Complete the upper half of the stitch by returning in the opposite direction, as shown in Diagram 3.

Cross-stitch can be worked in either direction, from right to left or left to right, but it is of the utmost importance that the upper half of each cross lies in the same direction.

Backstitch

Backstitch is used in many of the designs, mainly for outlines and finer details.

It is worked from hole to hole and can be stitched as a horizontal, diagonal or vertical line, as shown in Diagram 4.

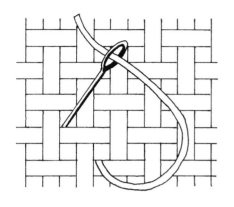

DIAGRAM 1

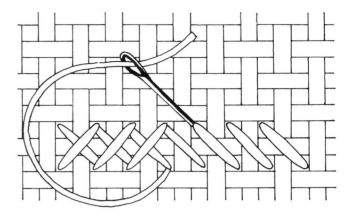

DIAGRAM 3

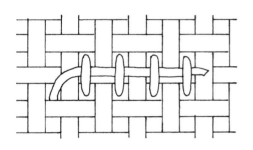

DIAGRAM 2

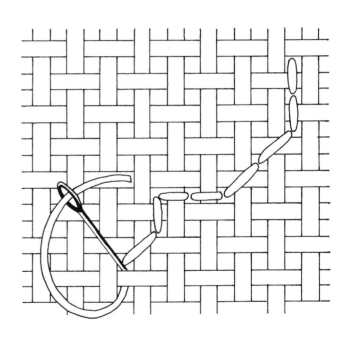

DIAGRAM 4

Materials

1 NEEDLES A small blunt tapestry needle, No. 24 or 26.

2 SCISSORS A sharp pair of embroidery scissors is essential.

3 EMBROIDERY HOOP A round, plastic or wooden hoop with a screw-type tension adjuster, 4 inches, 5 inches or 6 inches in diameter, is ideal for cross-stitch. Place the area of fabric to be embroidered over the inner ring and gently push the outer ring over it, ensuring that the fabric is taut and the mesh straight.

4 THREADS DMC six-strand embroidery cotton has been used to colour-code the designs in this book. The number of strands used will depend on the fabric you decide to work on.

5 FABRIC Do not use a fabric which does not have an even weave, as this will distort the embroidery either vertically or horizontally. An evenweave fabric on which it is easy to count the threads should be used. There are a few to choose from in varying thread counts. The most popular fabrics used are aida cloth, linen and hardanger cloth.
Cotton aida is available in the following sizes: 8, 11, 14 and 18 threads-per-inch.
Linen is available in the following sizes: 19/20, 25/26 and 30/31 threads-per-inch.
Hardanger is 22 threads-per-inch.

Preparing to work

To determine the size of the finished embroidery, count the squares on the chart for the entire width and depth of the design, and divide each by the number of threads-per-inch in the fabric you intend to use. This will give the dimensions in inches. Cut the fabric at least 2 inches wider each way than the finished size to allow for finishing. To prevent the fabric fraying, either machine-stitch or whip-stitch the outer edges or alternatively bind them with masking tape.

Find the centre of the fabric by folding it in half vertically and then horizontally. Mark the centre with a line of basting stitches both lengthwise and widthwise. Many of the charts in this book have arrows marking the vertical and horizontal centres. Follow these arrows to their intersection to locate the centre of the chart.

It is preferable to begin cross-stitch at the top of the design. To find the top, count the squares up from the centre of the chart and then the number of holes up from the centre of the fabric. Ensure that the fabric is held tautly in the embroidery hoop, as this makes stitching easier, enabling the needle to be pushed through the holes without piercing the fibres of the fabric.

If the fabric loosens while working, retighten as necessary. When working with stranded cotton, always separate the strands before threading the needle. This will give better coverage of the fabric.

The number of strands will depend on the fabric count that you use.

Finishing

When the embroidery is finished, it will need to be pressed. Place the finished work right side down on your ironing board, cover it with a thin, slightly dampened cloth, and iron.

If you intend to frame the finished embroidery yourself, you will need to block it. Cut a piece of board to the desired size and place the finished embroidery over it. Fold the surplus fabric to the back and secure along the top edge of the board with pins. Pull firmly over the opposite edge and pin in position.

Repeat along both side edges, pulling the fabric until it is lying taut on the board.

Secure at the back by lacing from side to side on all four sides with a strong thread. Remove the pins and frame as desired.

The Charted Designs

The breeds

The dog is Man's oldest and most versatile domestic animal. It can perform an almost endless variety of tasks, providing friendship and companionship to dog owners worldwide.

The breeds depicted in the following pages cover a wide range of the dog world from the Chihuahua to the Great Dane, enabling you to create an embroidery of your pet or your favourite dog.

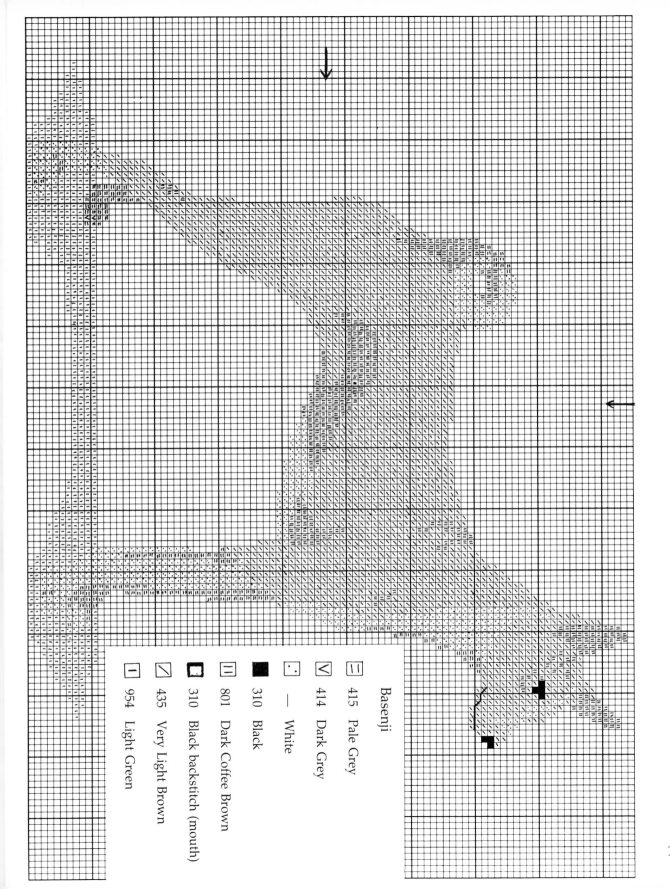

Basenji

⊟	415	Pale Grey
∨	414	Dark Grey
·	—	White
⊔	801	Dark Coffee Brown
■	310	Black
□	310	Black backstitch (mouth)
⬦	435	Very Light Brown
⊡	954	Light Green

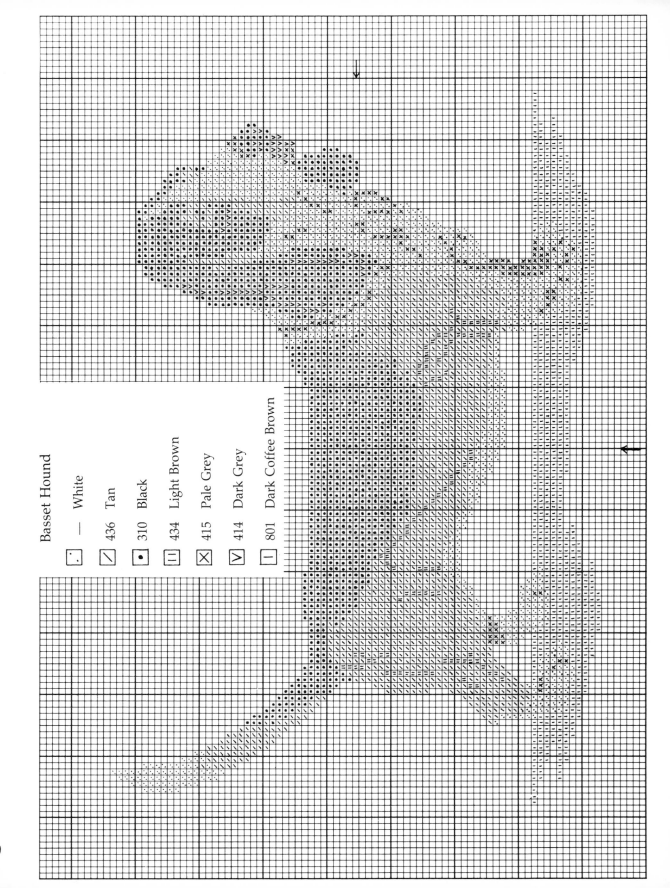

Basset Hound

⊡	—	White
⧄	436	Tan
●	310	Black
⊟	434	Light Brown
✕	415	Pale Grey
⋁	414	Dark Grey
⊟	801	Dark Coffee Brown

Beagle puppy and ball

⊡	321	Poppy Red
⊙	415	Pale Grey
⊿	—	White
⊠	898	Very Dark Coffee Brown
⊞	434	Light Brown
■	310	Black
⊡	436	Tan
⊽	413	Dark Pewter Grey
▢	310	Black backstitch (eyes)
⊐	801	Dark Coffee Brown
⊡	954	Light Green

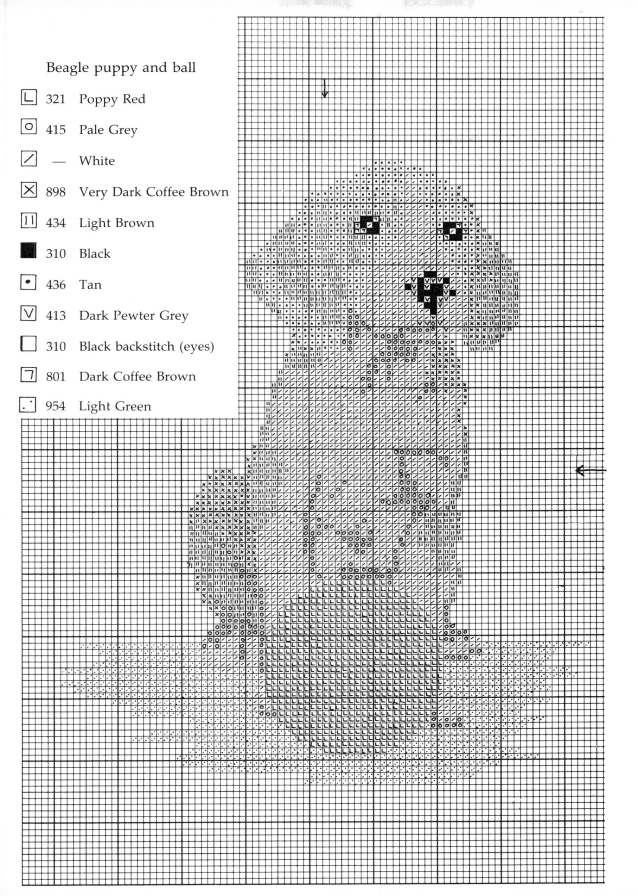

21

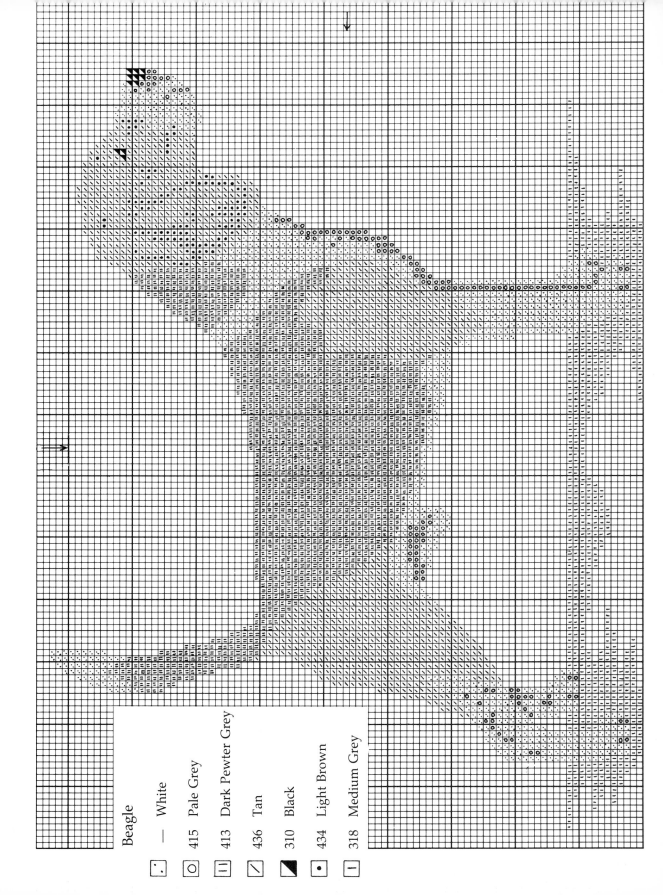

Beagle

		White
⬚∴	—	White
◯	415	Pale Grey
‖	413	Dark Pewter Grey
╱	436	Tan
◣	310	Black
•	434	Light Brown
−	318	Medium Grey

Bernese Mountain Dog

Symbol	Code	Color
C	919	Dark Copper
7	920	Medium Copper
V	413	Dark Pewter Grey
—	954	Light Green
·	-	White
O	921	Copper
II	414	Dark Grey
Z	310	Black
II	415	Pale Grey
L	818	Baby Pink
X	3326	Rose Pink
□	310	Black backstitch (nose)
□	318	Medium Grey backstitch (eyes)

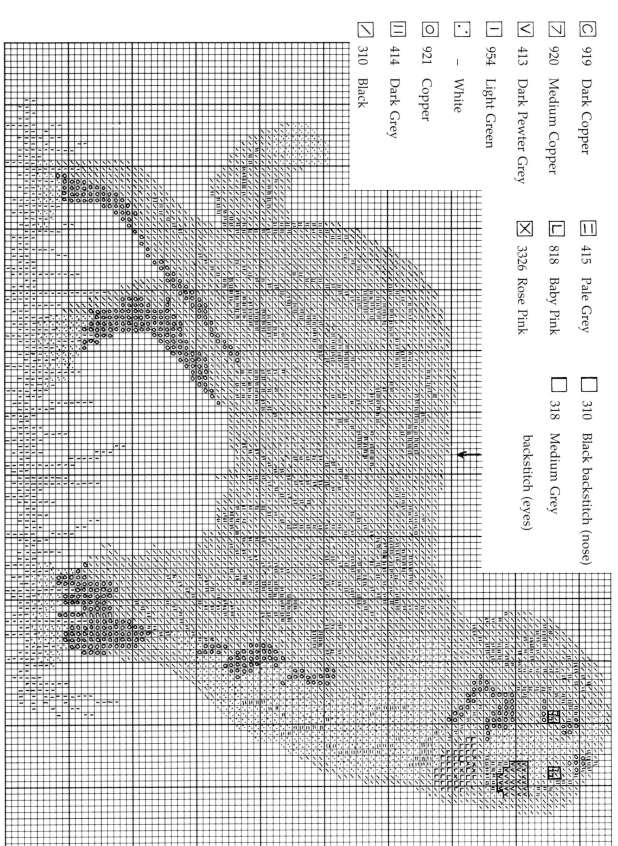

Border Collie

1	954 Light Green
:	— White
L	415 Pale Grey
■	801 Dark Coffee Brown

V	776 Medium Pink
	318 Medium Grey backstitch (eyes)
=	433 Medium Brown

/	310 Black
II	318 Medium Grey
O	818 Baby Pink
X	414 Dark Grey

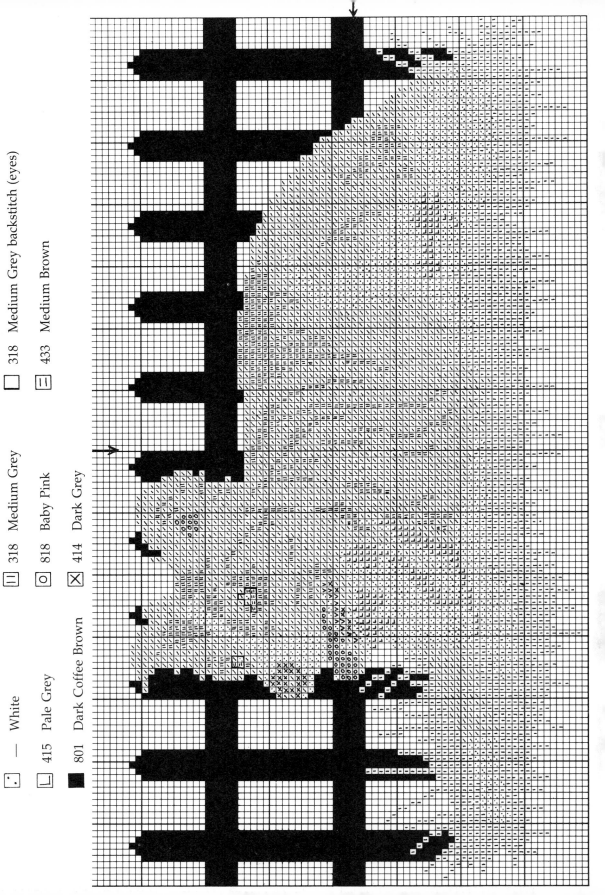

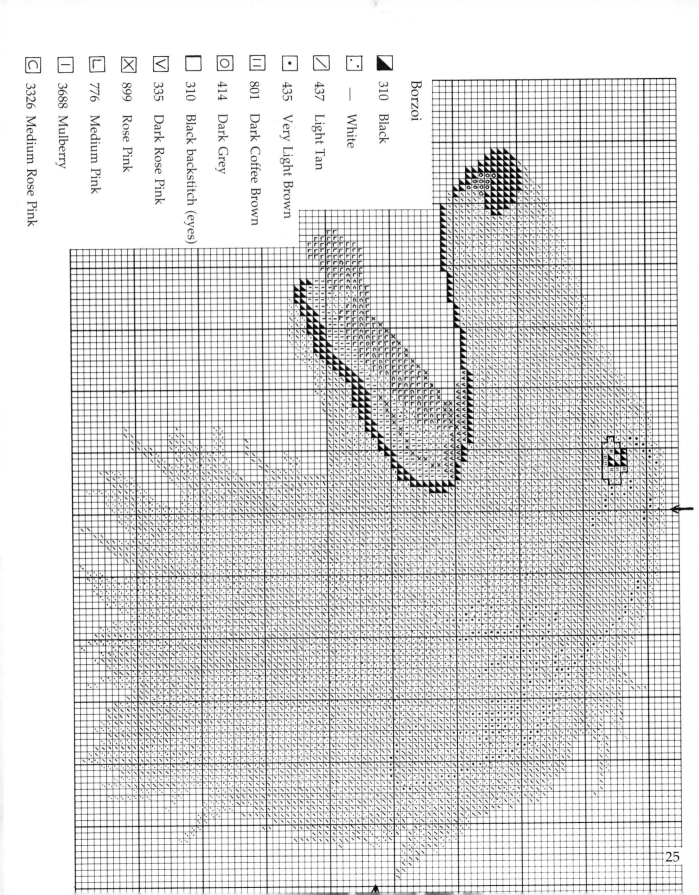

Borzoi

◪ 310 Black

⊡ — White

◪ 437 Light Tan

⊡ · 435 Very Light Brown

⊡ ▪ 801 Dark Coffee Brown

◉ 414 Dark Grey

☐ 310 Black backstitch (eyes)

✕ 335 Dark Rose Pink

▽ 899 Rose Pink

☒ 776 Medium Pink

⊟ 3688 Mulberry

© 3326 Medium Rose Pink

25

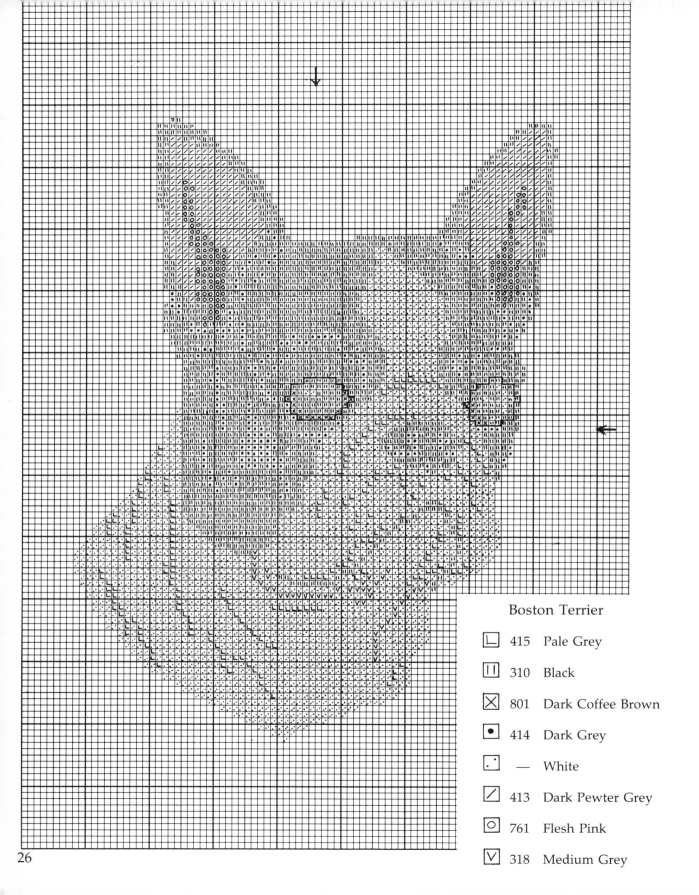

Boston Terrier

Symbol	Code	Colour
⌐	415	Pale Grey
‖	310	Black
⊠	801	Dark Coffee Brown
⊡	414	Dark Grey
—		White
╱	413	Dark Pewter Grey
⊙	761	Flesh Pink
⋁	318	Medium Grey

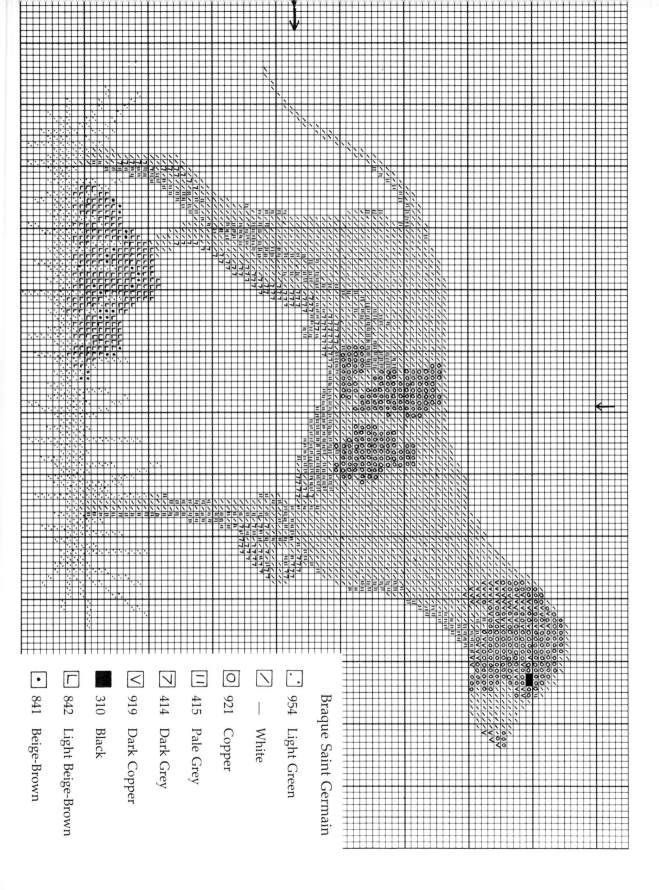

Braque Saint Germain

.	954	Light Green
/	—	White
O	921	Copper
II	415	Pale Grey
7	414	Dark Grey
V	919	Dark Copper
■	310	Black
L	842	Light Beige-Brown
•	841	Beige-Brown

Bull Terrier

☐	414	Dark Grey backstitch (eye)
Ⅱ	310	Black
⊙	414	Dark Grey
⊡	—	White
∟	415	Pale Grey
╱	818	Baby Pink
☒	760	Medium Flesh Pink
☑	413	Dark Pewter Grey
☑	433	Medium Brown

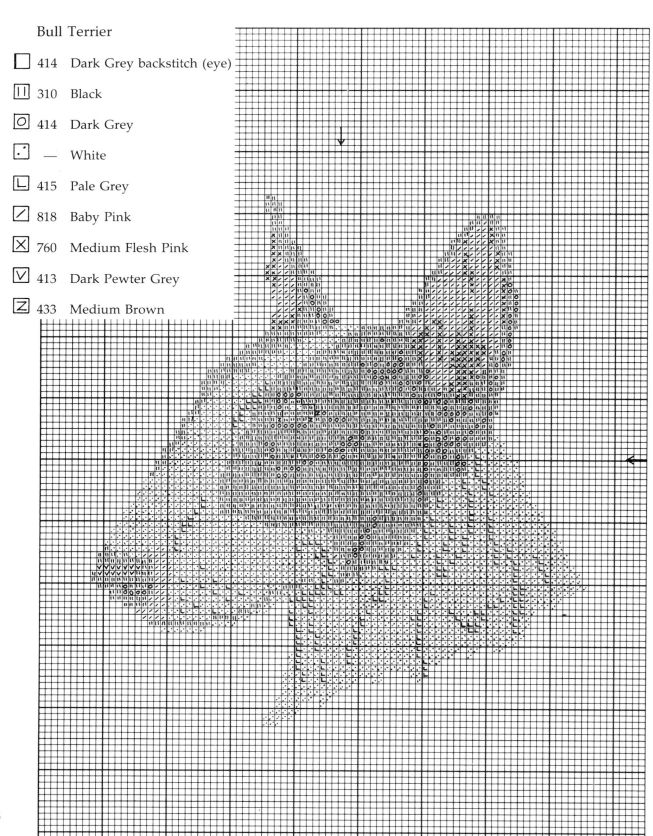

28

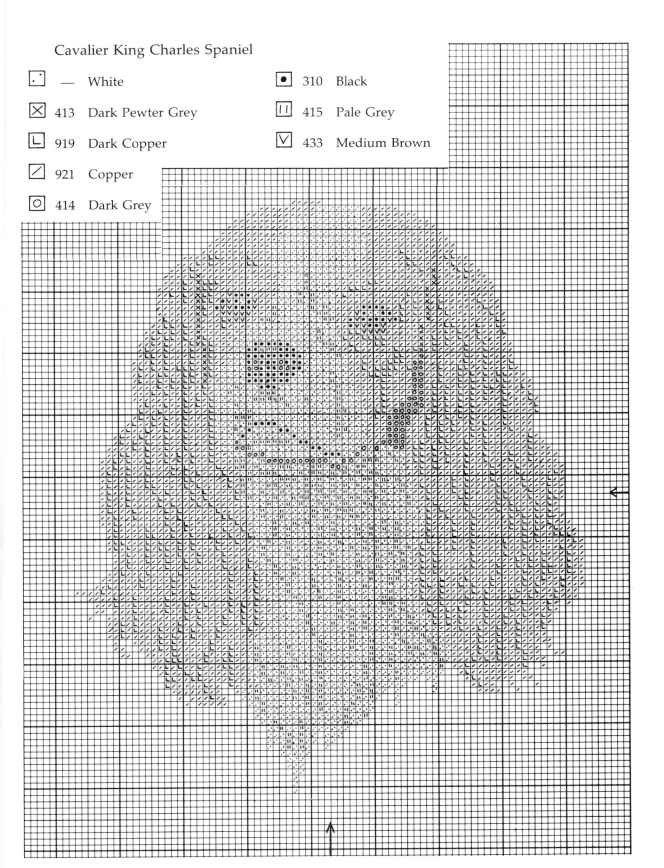

Cavalier King Charles Spaniel

Symbol	Code	Colour
⊡	—	White
⊠	413	Dark Pewter Grey
⌊	919	Dark Copper
⟋	921	Copper
⊙	414	Dark Grey
⊙	310	Black
∥	415	Pale Grey
⋁	433	Medium Brown

Chihuahua

- ▱ 436 Tan
- ▯ 435 Very Light Brown
- ◸ 310 Black
- ⋅ 738 Very Light Tan
- ▢ 414 Dark Grey
- • — White

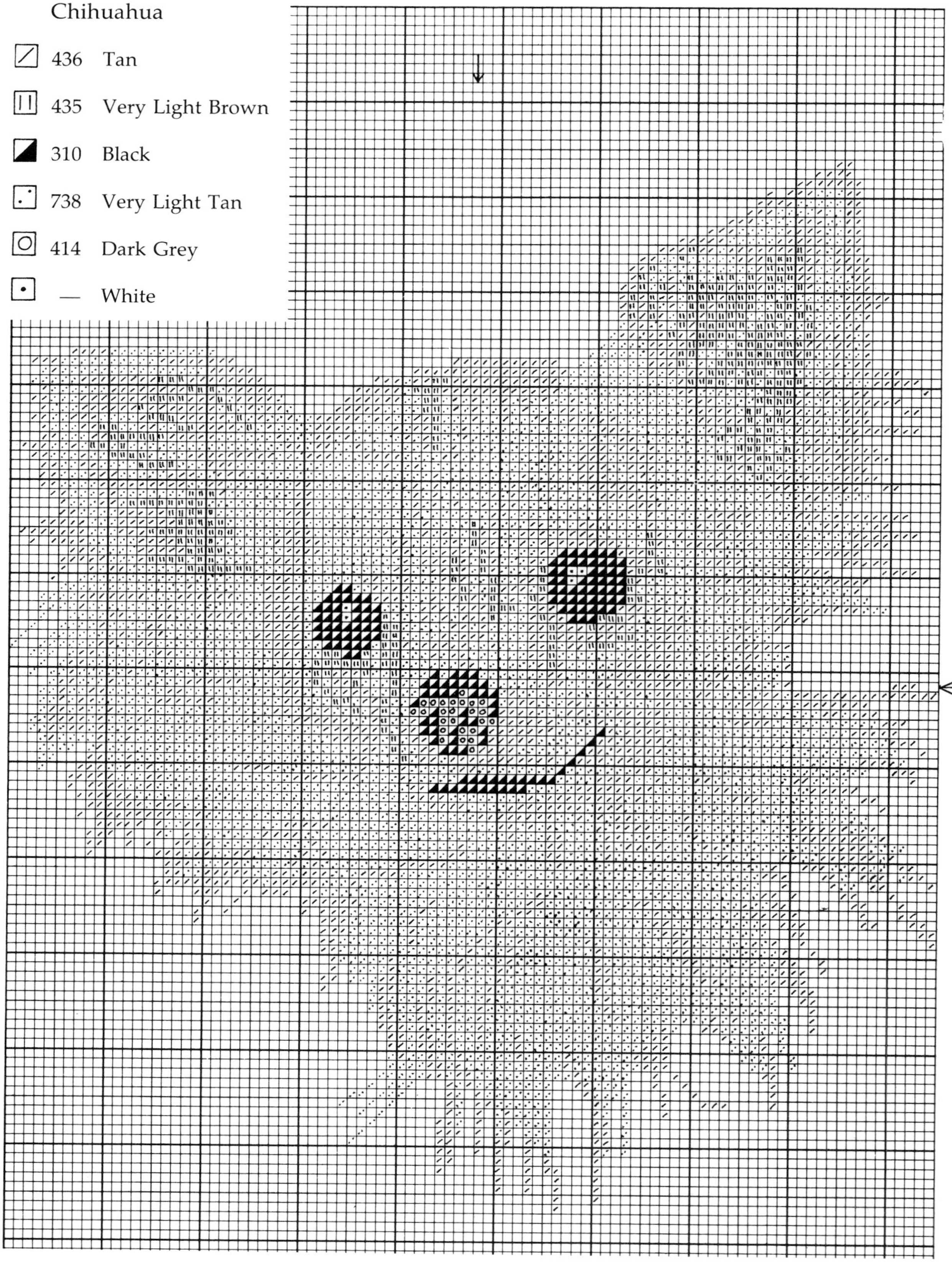

Chow-Chow

☒	801	Dark Coffee Brown	Ⅱ	434	Light Brown
⚬	738	Very Light Tan	∨	318	Medium Grey
⊙	—	Ecru	╱	436	Tan
⊡	310	Black	☰	919	Dark Copper
☐	310	Black backstitch (nose)	∟	334	Medium Baby Blue
7	413	Dark Pewter Grey	∧	312	Dark Blue

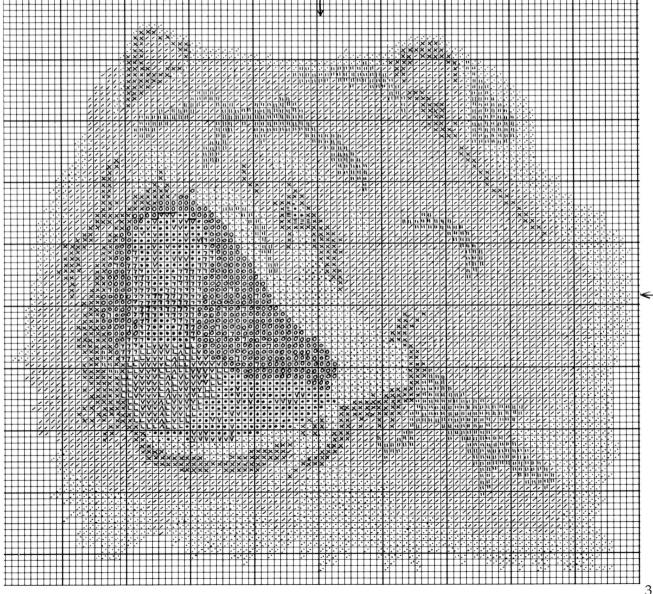

31

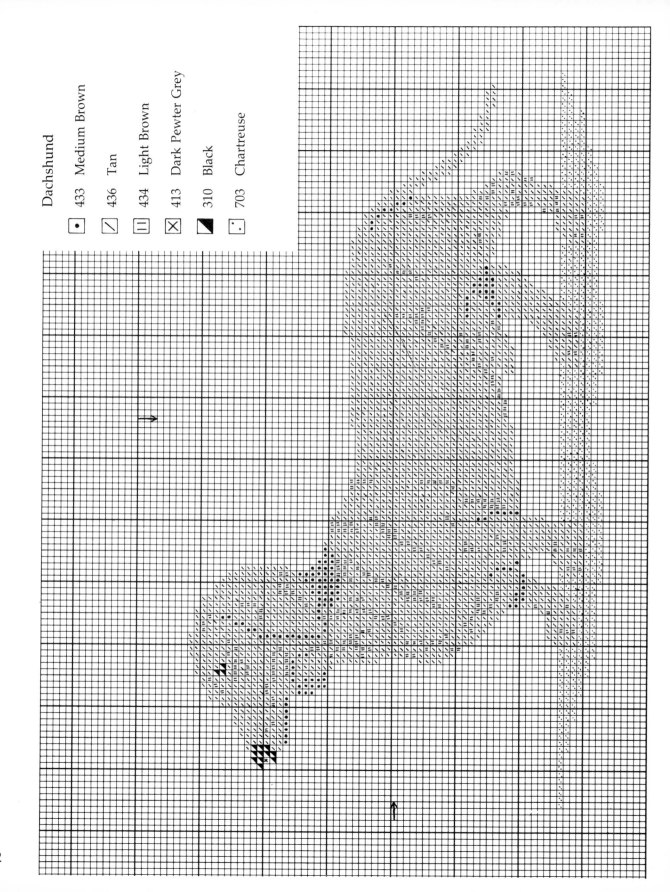

Dachshund

	433	Medium Brown
•	433	Medium Brown
/	436	Tan
I I	434	Light Brown
X	413	Dark Pewter Grey
◣	310	Black
:	703	Chartreuse

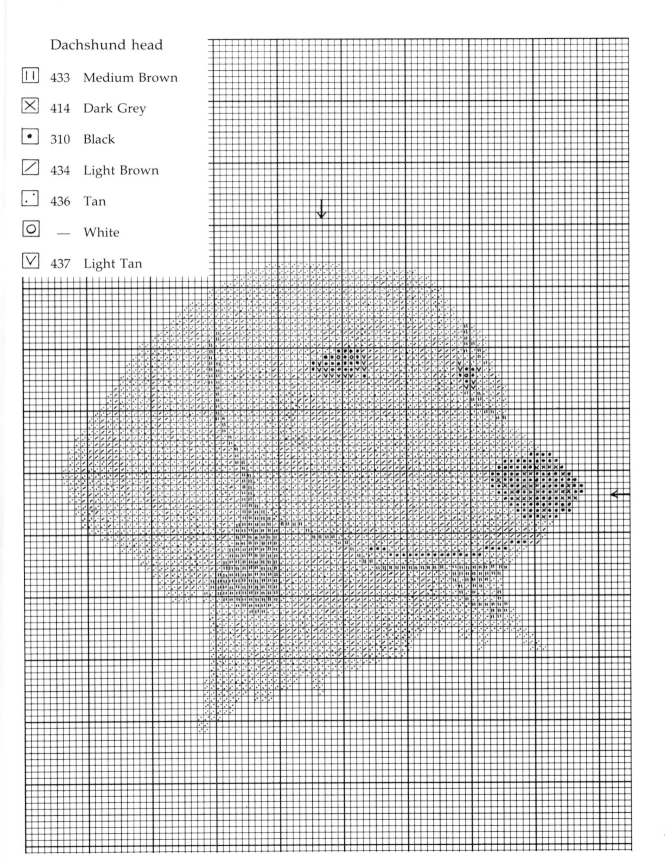

Dachshund head

	433	Medium Brown
	414	Dark Grey
	310	Black
	434	Light Brown
	436	Tan
	—	White
	437	Light Tan

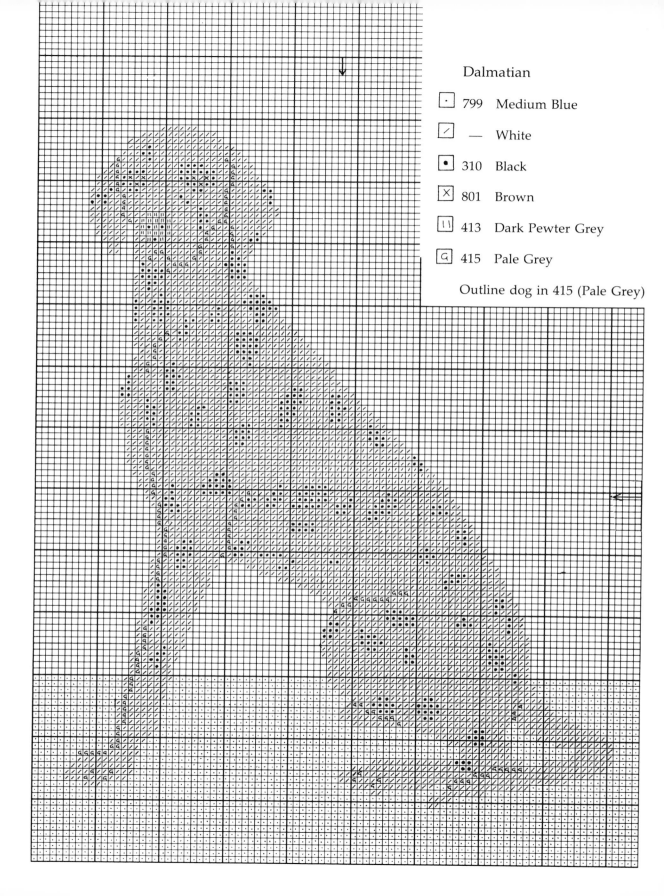

Dalmatian

⊡	799	Medium Blue
╱	—	White
⊙	310	Black
☒	801	Brown
⊍	413	Dark Pewter Grey
Ḡ	415	Pale Grey

Outline dog in 415 (Pale Grey)

Dalmatian head

●	310	Black
∴	—	White
II	415	Pale Grey
✕	414	Dark Grey
V	433	Medium Brown
☐	310	Black backstitch (eyes)

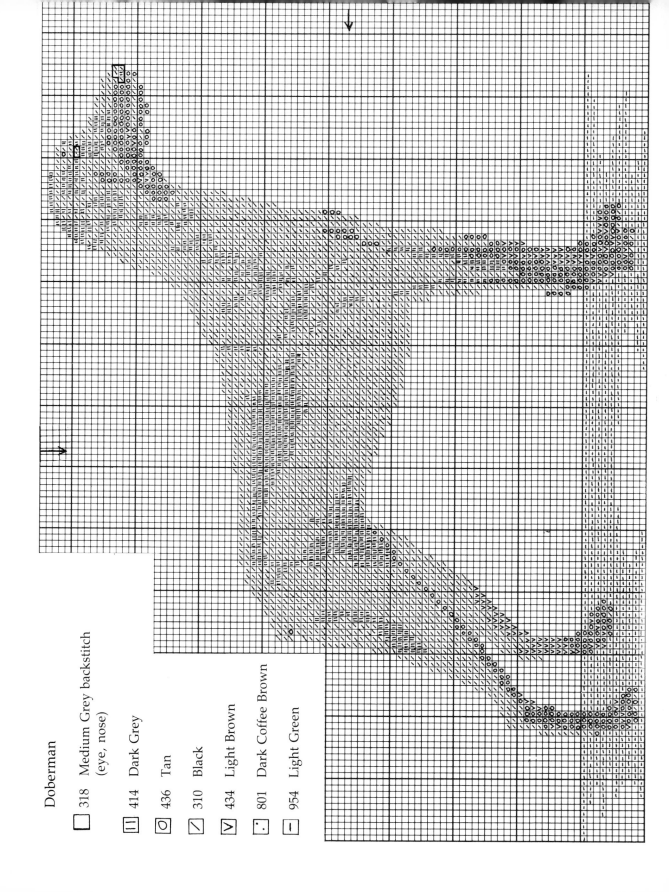

Doberman

	318	Medium Grey backstitch (eye, nose)
[I]	414	Dark Grey
[O]	436	Tan
[/]	310	Black
[V]	434	Light Brown
[:]	801	Dark Coffee Brown
[-]	954	Light Green

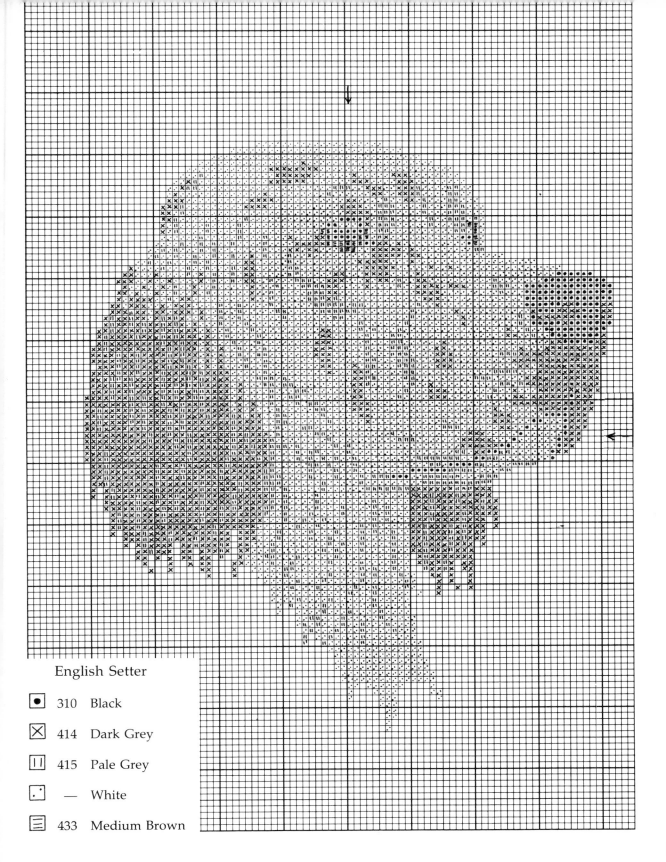

English Setter

●	310	Black
☒	414	Dark Grey
‖	415	Pale Grey
∴	—	White
☰	433	Medium Brown

Eurasier

•	898	Medium Dark Coffee Brown			■	310	Black
⊡	—	Ecru			⊠	413	Dark Pewter Grey
I I	921	Copper			Z	318	Medium Grey
╱	738	Very Light Tan			V	776	Medium Pink
7	434	Light Brown			Γ	899	Rose Pink
L	436	Tan			I	954	Light Green

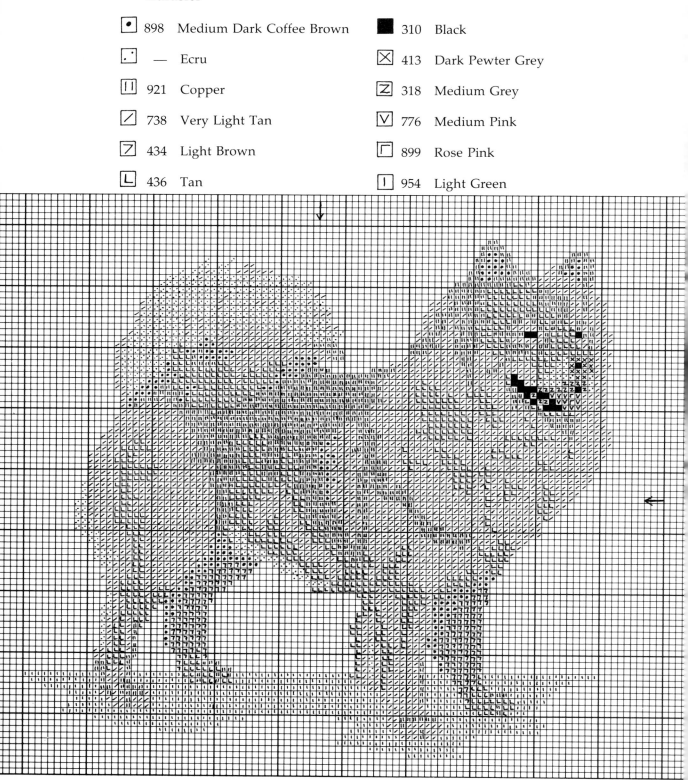

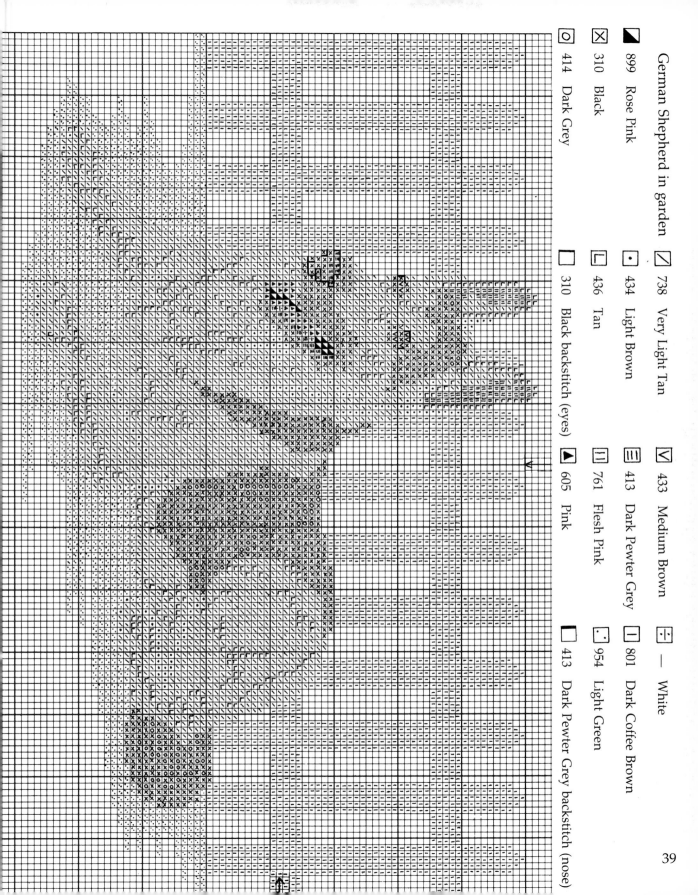

German Shepherd in garden

Symbol	Code	Color
◩	738	Very Light Tan
◪	433	Medium Brown
⊡	—	White
◨	899	Rose Pink
·	434	Light Brown
⊞	413	Dark Pewter Grey
⊟	801	Dark Coffee Brown
⊠	310	Black
◰	436	Tan
⊡	761	Flesh Pink
⊡	954	Light Green
○	414	Dark Grey
□	310	Black backstitch (eyes)
▲	605	Pink
□	413	Dark Pewter Grey backstitch (nose)

German Shepherd head

•	310	Black	
III	433	Medium Brown	
I	—	White	
=	318	Medium Grey	
V	414	Dark Grey	
/	436	Tan	
II	434	Light Brown	
⠒	738	Very Light Tan	
O	642	Fawn	
X	761	Flesh Pink	

◢	902	Very Deep Red
◠	760	Medium Flesh Pink
◻	414	Dark Grey backstitch (eye)

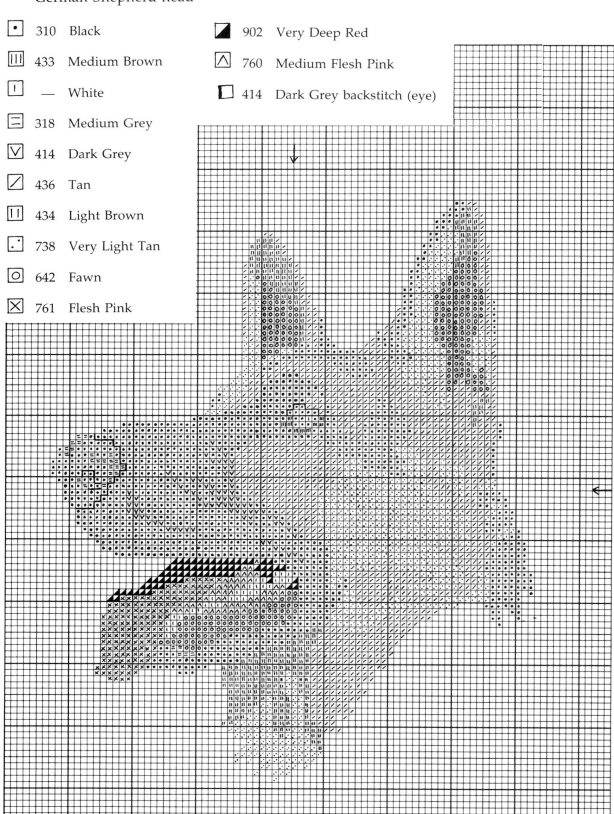

Golden Cocker Spaniel puppy with slipper

⟋	437	Light Tan
▲	435	Very Light Brown
☰	433	Medium Brown
·	436	Tan
○	826	Blue
‖	813	Light Blue
Z	796	Dark Royal Blue
⠂	783	Christmas Gold
V	434	Light Brown
X	738	Very Light Tan
⁒	413	Dark Pewter Grey
■	310	Black

◣	801	Dark Coffee Brown
◾	—	White
I	797	Royal Blue

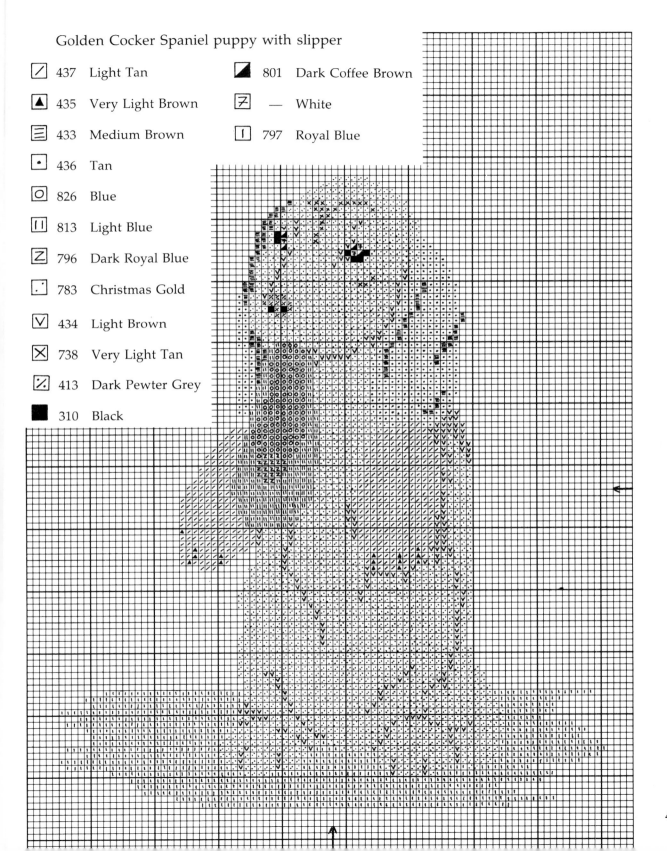

Golden Retriever

Symbol	Code	Name
◿	738	Very Light Tan
◢	310	Black
⊡	—	White
⊙	801	Dark Coffee Brown
⊠	436	Tan
⊡	434	Light Brown
⊞	414	Dark Grey

Great Dane

L	818	Baby Pink	O	3326	Rose Pink	
•	310	Black	C	776	Medium Pink	
X	414	Dark Grey	T	335	Deep Rose Pink	
II	436	Tan				
/	738	Very Light Tan				
≡	434	Light Brown				
V	435	Very Light Brown				
Z	433	Medium Brown				
∴	—	White				

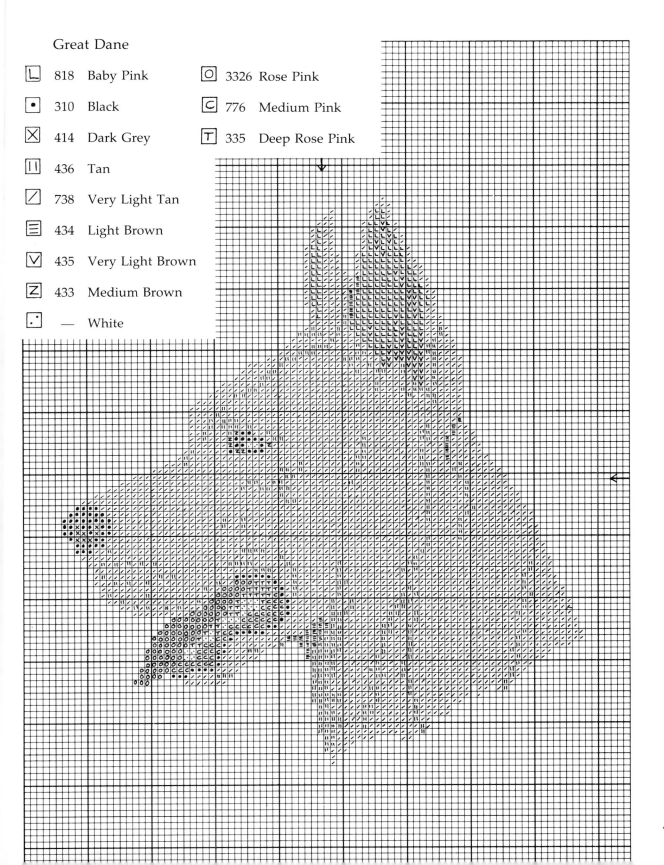

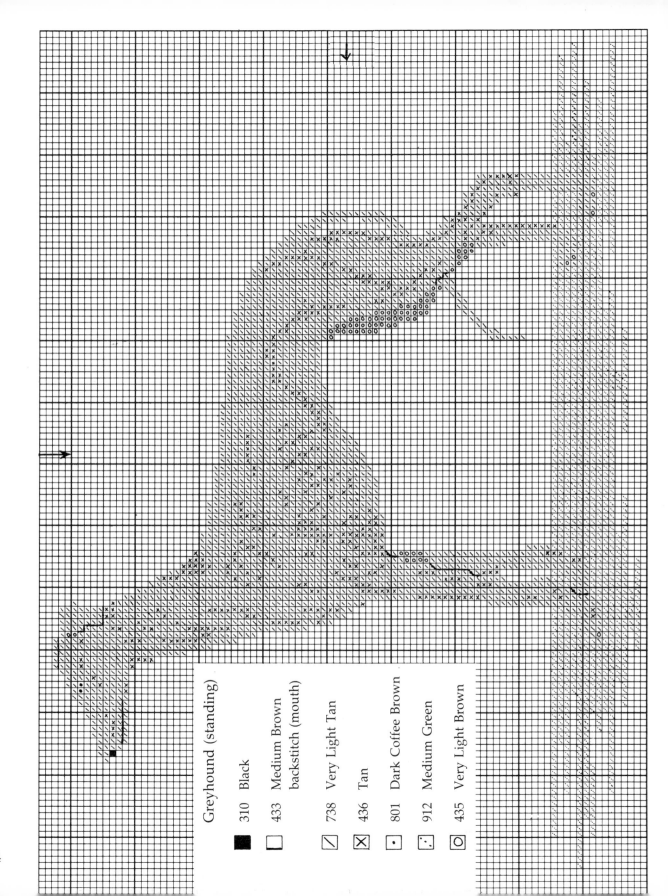

Greyhound (standing)

■	310	Black
□	433	Medium Brown backstitch (mouth)
⁄	738	Very Light Tan
✕	436	Tan
·	801	Dark Coffee Brown
∴	912	Medium Green
○	435	Very Light Brown

Greyhound head

—	White	
·	437	Light Tan
☐	414	Dark Grey backstitch (mouth)
Z	310	Black
III	414	Dark Grey
O	435	Very Light Brown
V	938	Very Dark Coffee Brown
X	801	Dark Coffee Brown
■	436	Tan
⟋	738	Very Light Tan
•	3688	Mulberry
L	776	Medium Pink
II	3687	Medium Mulberry

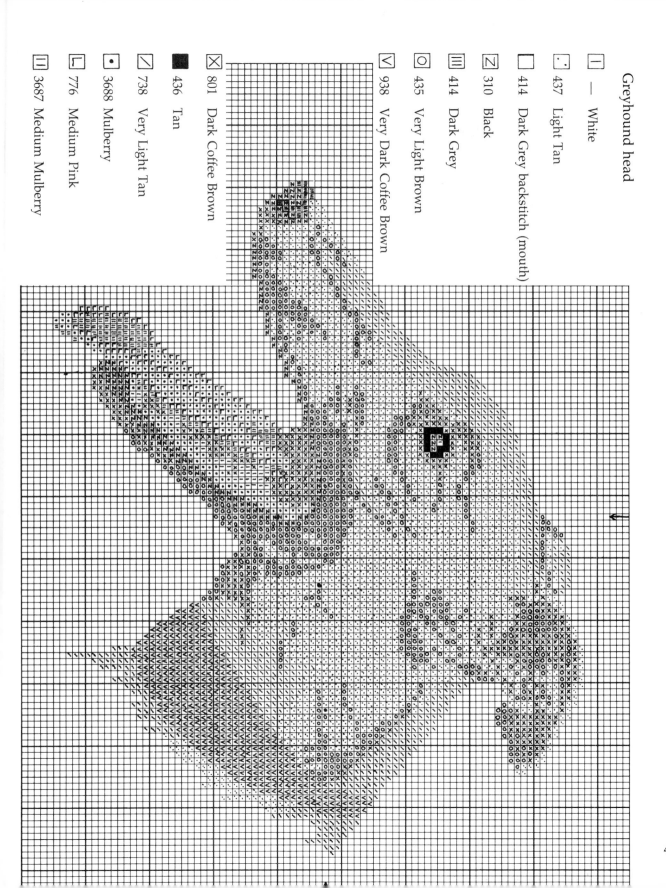

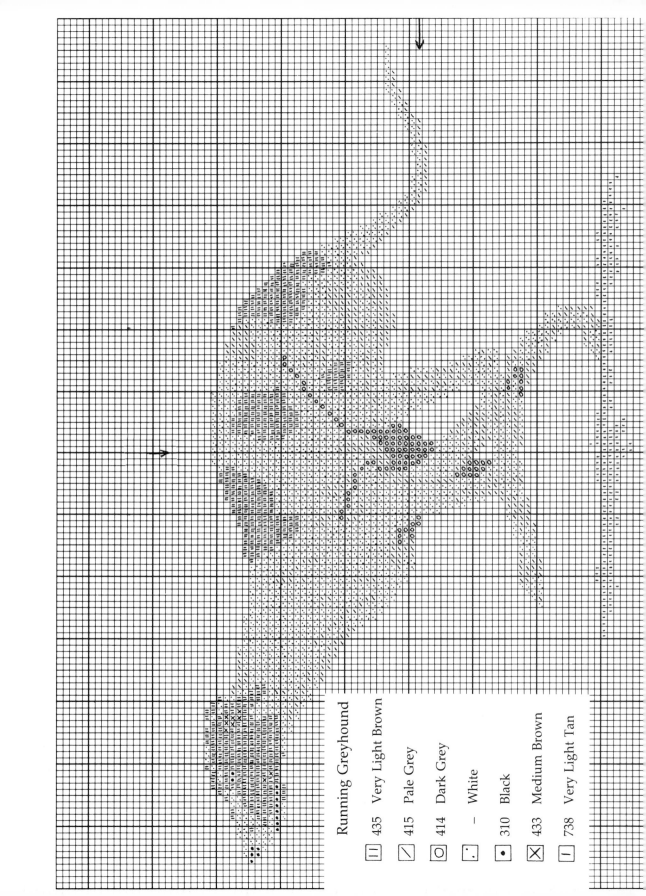

Running Greyhound

		435	Very Light Brown
/	415	Pale Grey
O	414	Dark Grey
.·	–	White
•	310	Black
X	433	Medium Brown
I	738	Very Light Tan

Jack Russell

Symbol	Code	Colour
.	954	Light Green
O	433	Medium Brown
/	—	White
|1	415	Pale Grey
•	310	Black
	318	Medium Grey backstitch (muzzle)
Z	414	Dark Grey
L	436	Tan
☰	318	Medium Grey
V	898	Medium Dark Coffee Brown
	310	Black backstitch (eyes)

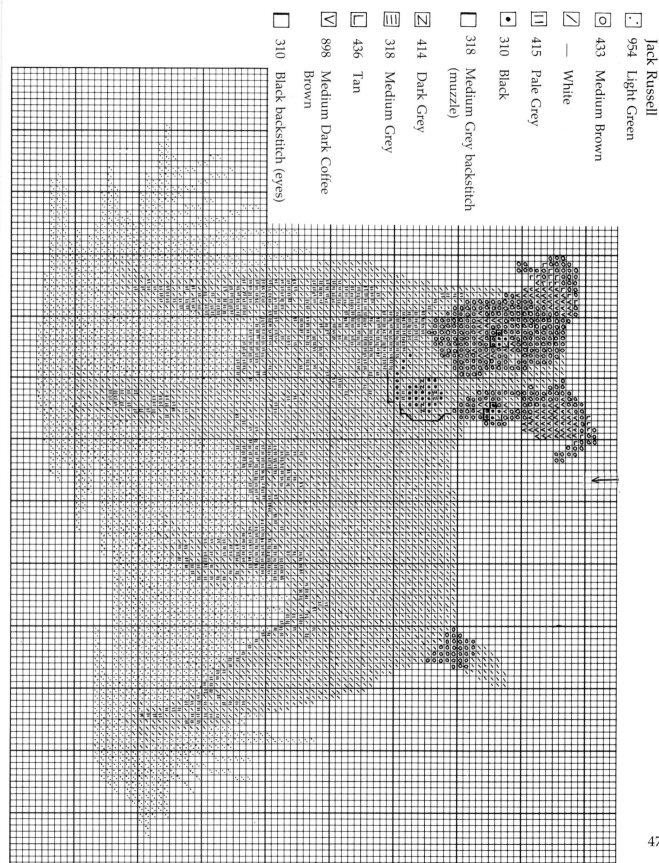

47

Maltese

⟋ 415 Pale Grey	⊡ — White	
☒ 318 Medium Grey	⊡ 776 Medium Pink	
■ 310 Black		

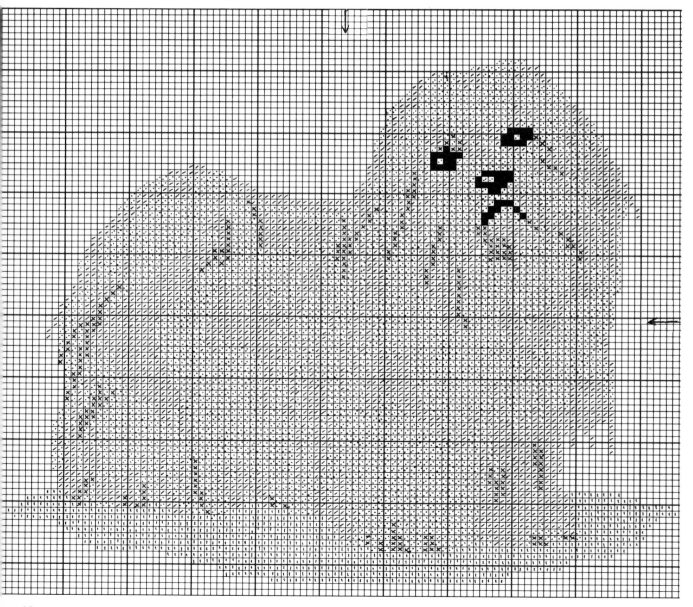

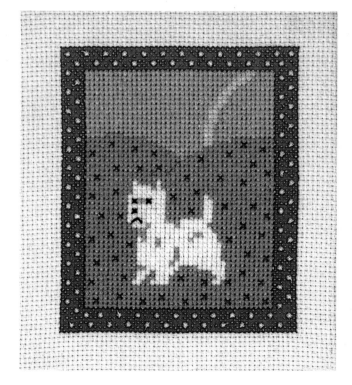

Poodle

☑	415	Pale Grey
⊡	310	Black
☒	414	Dark Grey
⊞	318	Medium Grey
◩	—	White
⬭	433	Medium Brown

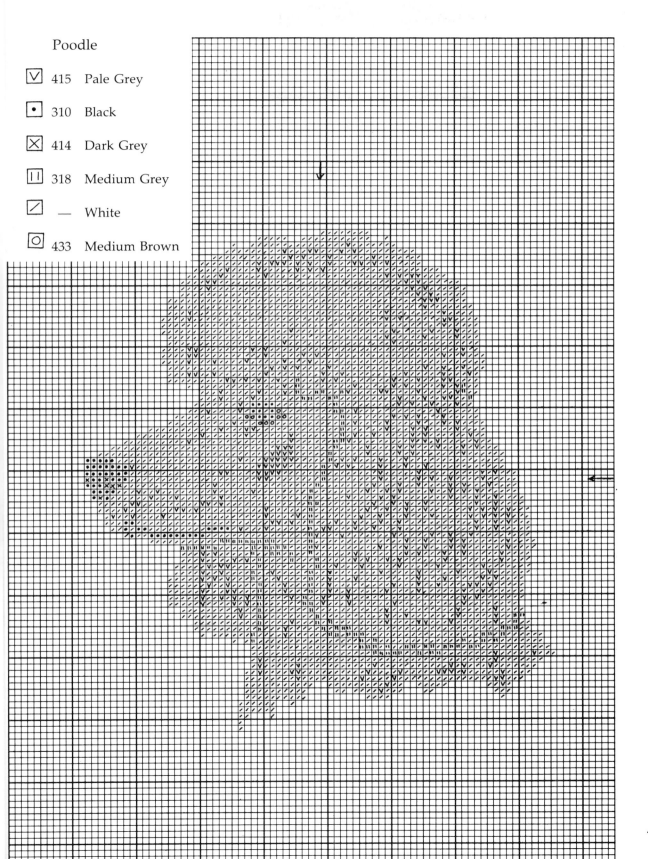

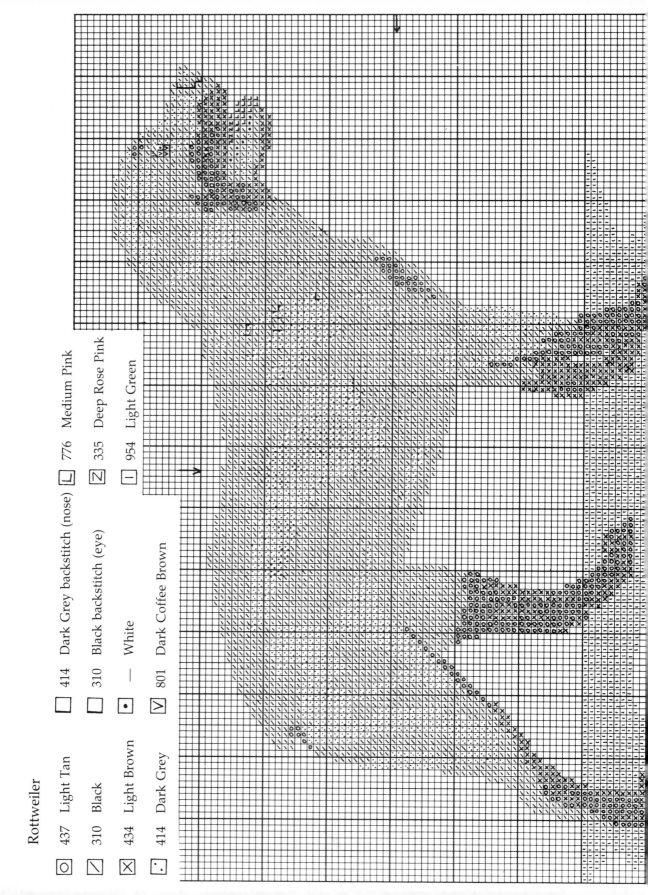

Rottweiler

Symbol	Code	Name
◎	437	Light Tan
⧄	310	Black
✕	434	Light Brown
⫶	414	Dark Grey
▱	414	Dark Grey backstitch (nose)
▱	310	Black backstitch (eye)
•	—	White
▽	801	Dark Coffee Brown
L	776	Medium Pink
Z	335	Deep Rose Pink
I	954	Light Green

Rough Collie

◣	433	Medium Brown
✕	801	Dark Coffee Brown
∴	—	White
Ⅱ	415	Pale Grey
●	310	Black
⊿	413	Dark Pewter Grey
╱	738	Very Light Tan
�“	436	Tan
☰	434	Light Brown
☑	335	Deep Rose Pink
⊟	3326	Rose Pink
◢	318	Medium Grey

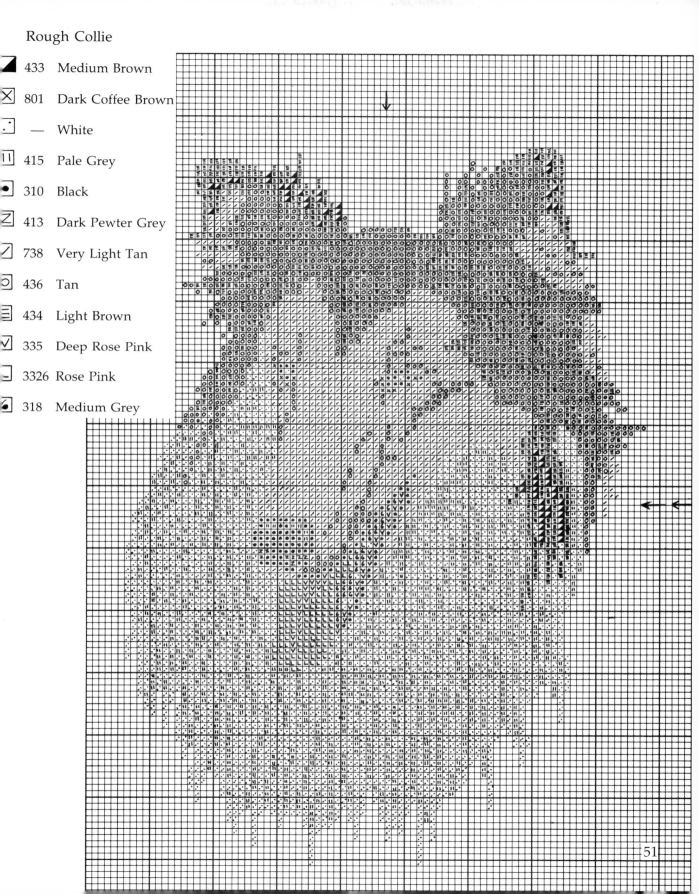

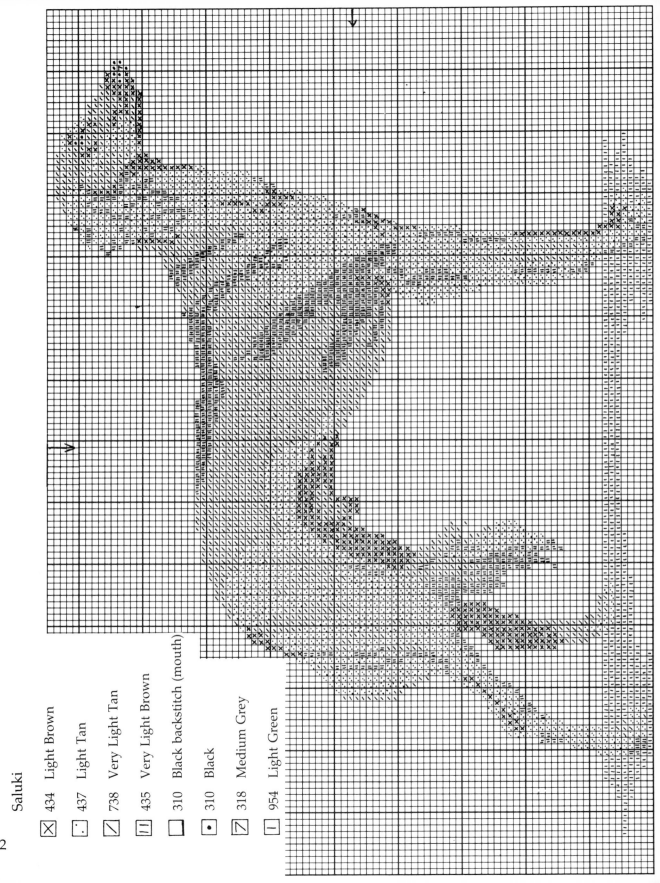

Saluki

☒	434	Light Brown
⠌	437	Light Tan
╱	738	Very Light Tan
‖	435	Very Light Brown
☐	310	Black backstitch (mouth)
•	310	Black
╲	318	Medium Grey
│	954	Light Green

52

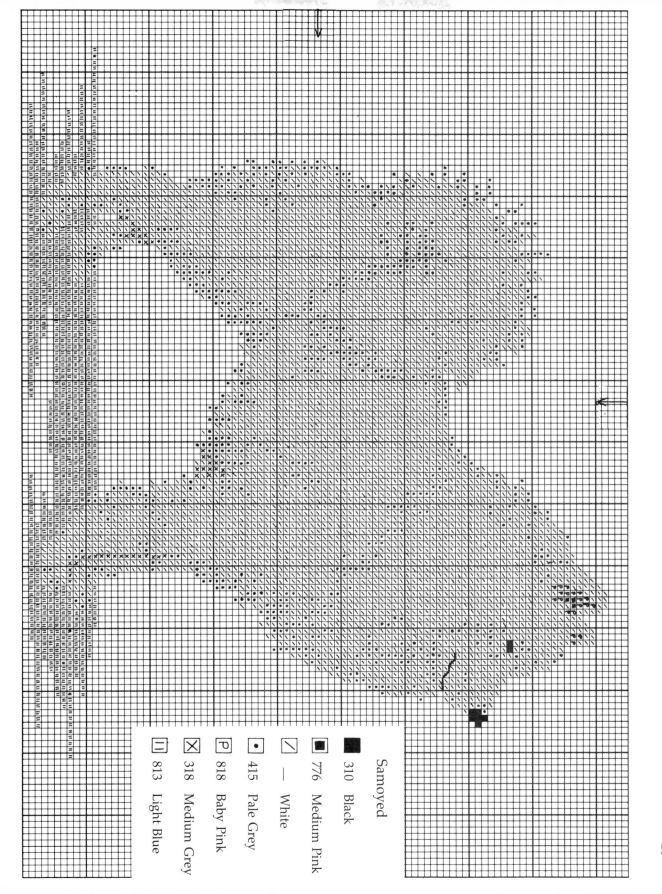

	Samoyed
■	310 Black
◼	776 Medium Pink
╱	— White
•	415 Pale Grey
P	818 Baby Pink
X	318 Medium Grey
I	813 Light Blue

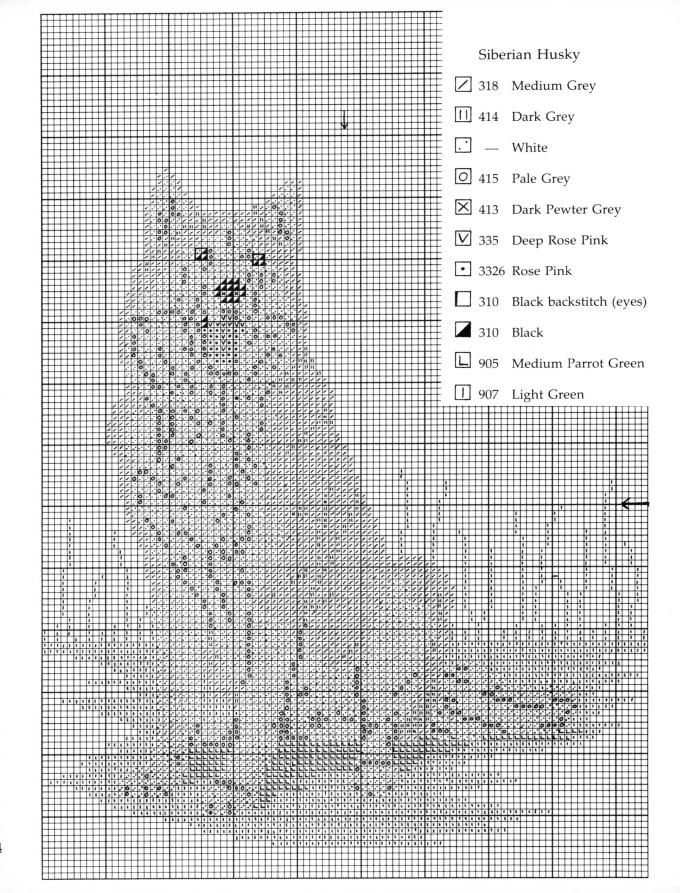

Siberian Husky

╱	318	Medium Grey
‖	414	Dark Grey
·	—	White
O	415	Pale Grey
✕	413	Dark Pewter Grey
V	335	Deep Rose Pink
•	3326	Rose Pink
□	310	Black backstitch (eyes)
◣	310	Black
L	905	Medium Parrot Green
I	907	Light Green

Springer Spaniel

⊡	801	Dark Coffee Brown	⊠	435	Very Light Brown
⊙	434	Light Brown	⊡	738	Very Light Tan
⊘	—	White	◣	898	Medium Dark Coffee Brown
⊞	415	Pale Grey			
☐	801	Dark Coffee Brown backstitch (mouth)			

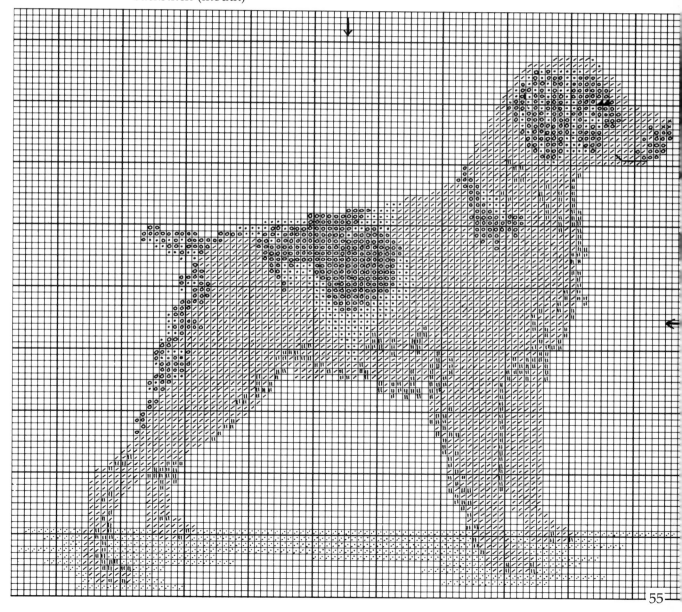

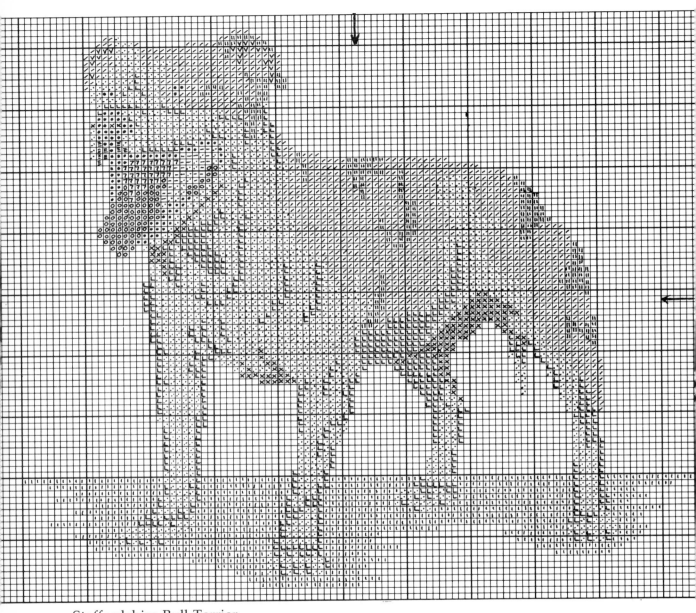

Staffordshire Bull Terrier

L	415	Pale Grey	V	801	Dark Coffee Brown	—	3688 Light Mulberry
⊡	—	White	●	310	Black	I	954 Light Green
⁄	436	Tan	O	776	Medium Pink	X	414 Dark Grey
II	434	Light Brown	☰	413	Dark Pewter Grey	Z	899 Rose Pink

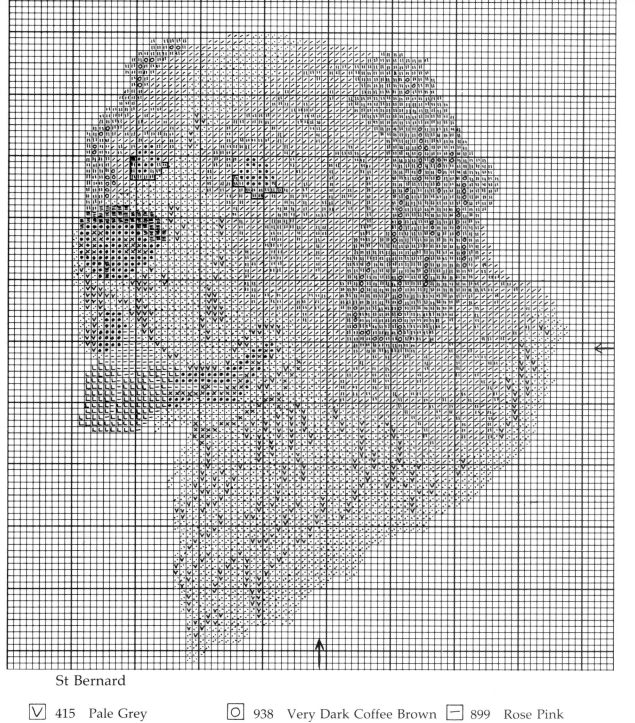

St Bernard

$\boxed{V}$ 415 Pale Grey	$\boxed{O}$ 938 Very Dark Coffee Brown	$\boxed{-}$ 899 Rose Pink
$\boxed{X}$ 318 Medium Grey	$\boxed{\bullet}$ 310 Black	$\boxed{}$ 310 Black backstitch (eyes)
$\boxed{\cdot}$ — White	$\boxed{\equiv}$ 413 Dark Pewter Grey	$\boxed{||}$ 801 Dark Coffee Brown
$\boxed{/}$ 434 Light Brown	$\boxed{L}$ 776 Medium Pink	

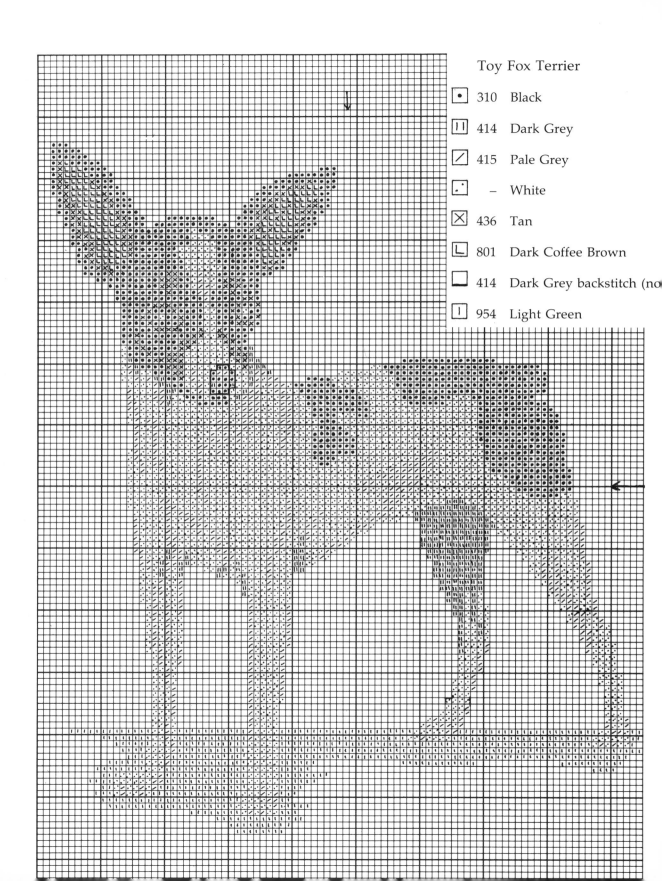

Toy Fox Terrier

•	310	Black
I I	414	Dark Grey
/	415	Pale Grey
.	–	White
X	436	Tan
L	801	Dark Coffee Brown
☐	414	Dark Grey backstitch (no
I	954	Light Green

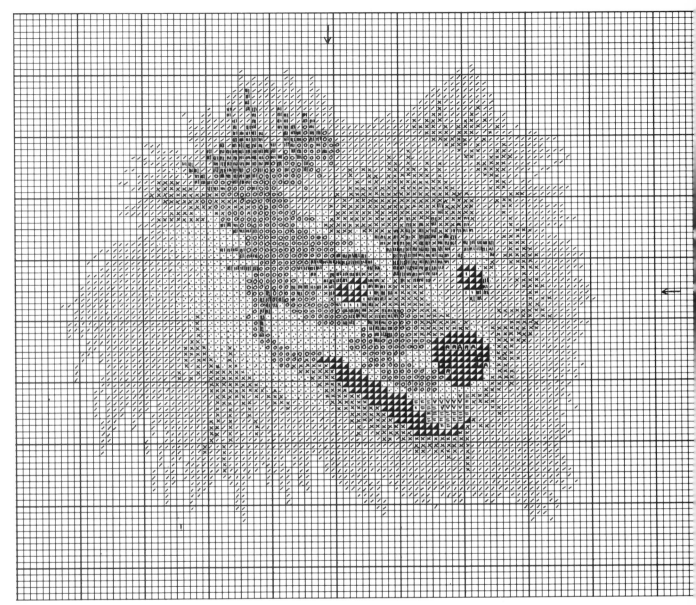

Toy Spitz

⊠	435	Very Light Brown	⊟	776	Medium Pink
⫼	801	Dark Coffee Brown	�	899	Rose Pink
·.	738	Very Light Tan	Ⓐ	318	Medium Grey
⁄	437	Light Tan	ⓞ	436	Tan
Ⅰ	—	White	◪	310	Black

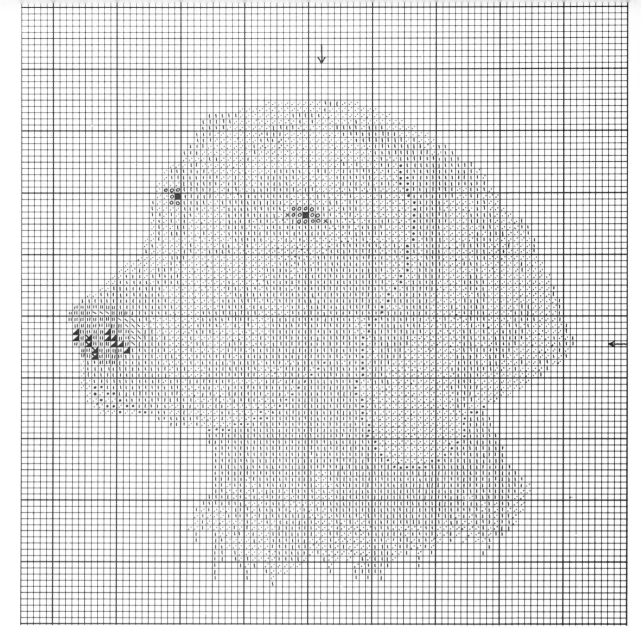

Weimaraner

◤	938	Very Dark Coffee Brown	⊡ 437	Light Tan
⊠	435	Very Light Brown	■ 310	Black
Ⅰ	642	Fawn	◥ 898	Medium Dark Coffee Brown
⊡	841	Beige-Brown	‖ 801	Dark Coffee Brown
⊡	644	Very Light Fawn	� 433	Medium Brown

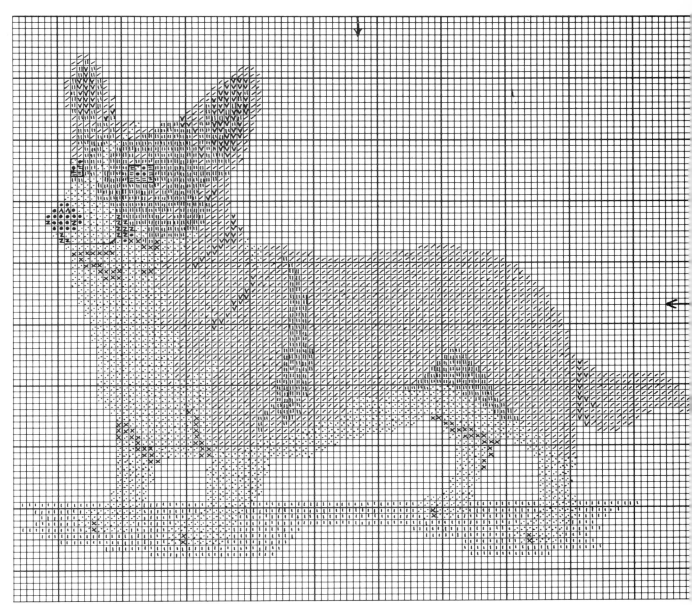

Welsh Corgi

Symbol	Code	Color
⋅	—	White
X	415	Pale Grey
•	310	Black
╱	436	Tan
V	434	Light Brown
II	738	Very Light Tan
⊟	433	Medium Brown
☐	310	Black backstitch (eyes, mouth)
Z	413	Dark Pewter Grey
Λ	318	Medium Grey
I	954	Light Green

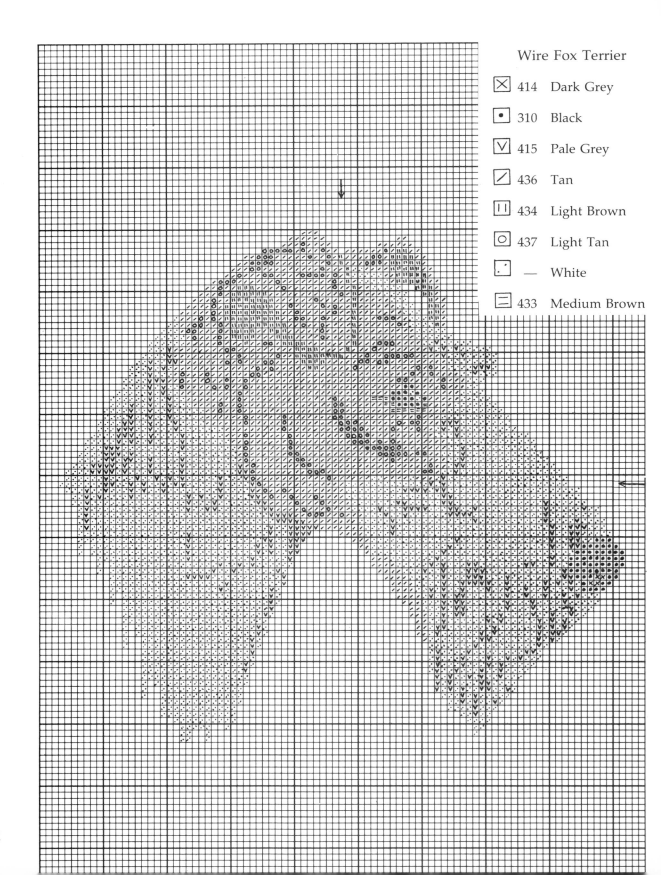

Wire Fox Terrier

☒	414	Dark Grey
⊡	310	Black
⊻	415	Pale Grey
⧄	436	Tan
⫲	434	Light Brown
⊙	437	Light Tan
⊡	—	White
⊟	433	Medium Brown

Yellow Labrador puppy with ball

☐	827	Sky Blue	◹	954	Light Green
2	—	White	⊙	444	Yellow
·	738	Very Light Tan	◤	742	Amber
◈	436	Tan	⊟	776	Pink
◿	801	Dark Coffee Brown	⏽	554	Lilac
S	310	Black	◼	414	Dark Grey

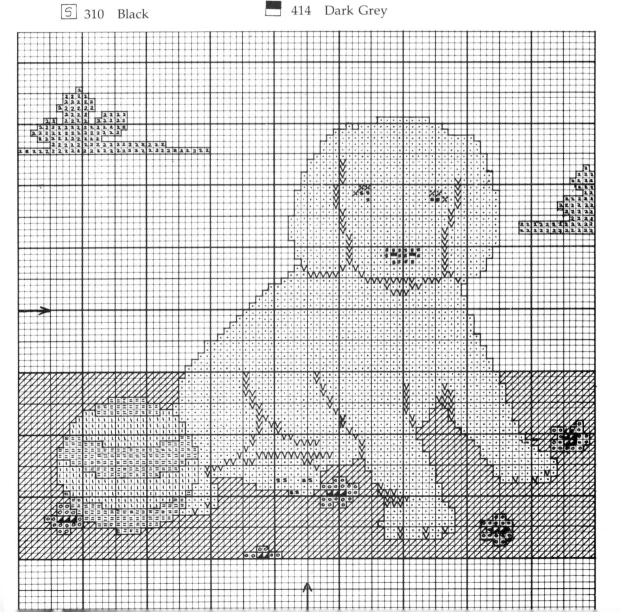

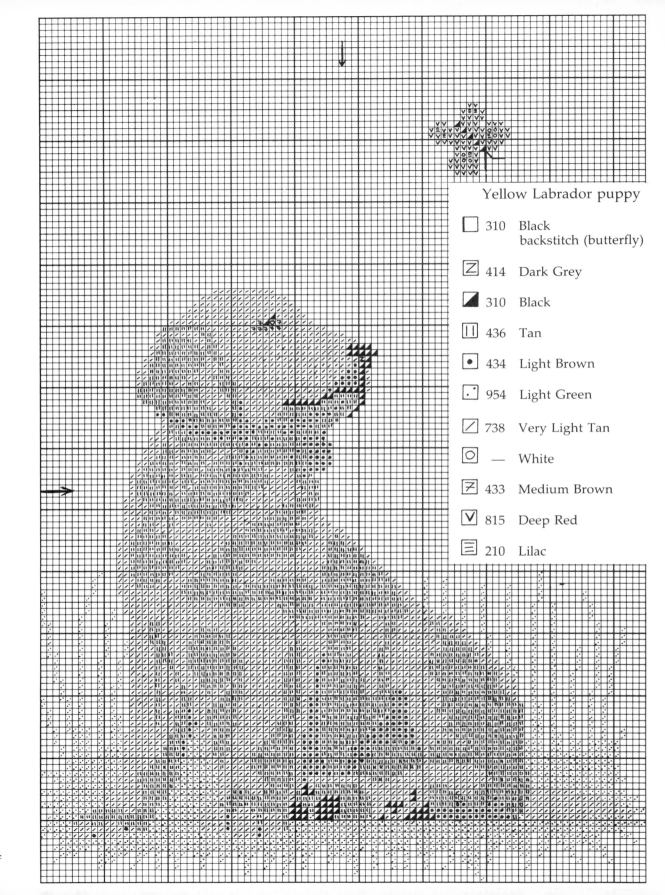

Yellow Labrador puppy

Symbol	Code	Color
□	310	Black backstitch (butterfly)
☑	414	Dark Grey
◤	310	Black
‖	436	Tan
•	434	Light Brown
⋮	954	Light Green
╱	738	Very Light Tan
O	—	White
⌐	433	Medium Brown
V	815	Deep Red
☰	210	Lilac

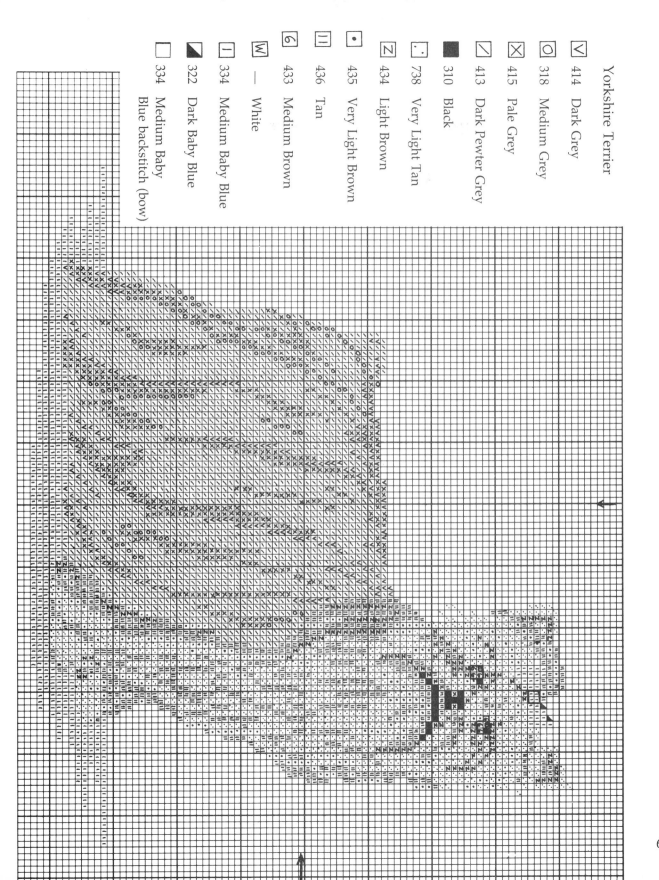

Yorkshire Terrier

Symbol	Code	Color
V	414	Dark Grey
O	318	Medium Grey
X	415	Pale Grey
/	413	Dark Pewter Grey
■	310	Black
.	738	Very Light Tan
Z	434	Light Brown
.	435	Very Light Brown
I	436	Tan
6	433	Medium Brown
—		White
W	334	Medium Baby Blue
◣	322	Dark Baby Blue
□	334	Medium Baby Blue backstitch (bow)

Decorative panels and borders

The following designs can be used for wall-hangings or decorative panels. The border designs can be used to add a distinctive touch to tablecloths, table runners, bedclothes or children's clothes.

The four miniature designs can be stitched as a set of four separate designs or grouped together as one design.

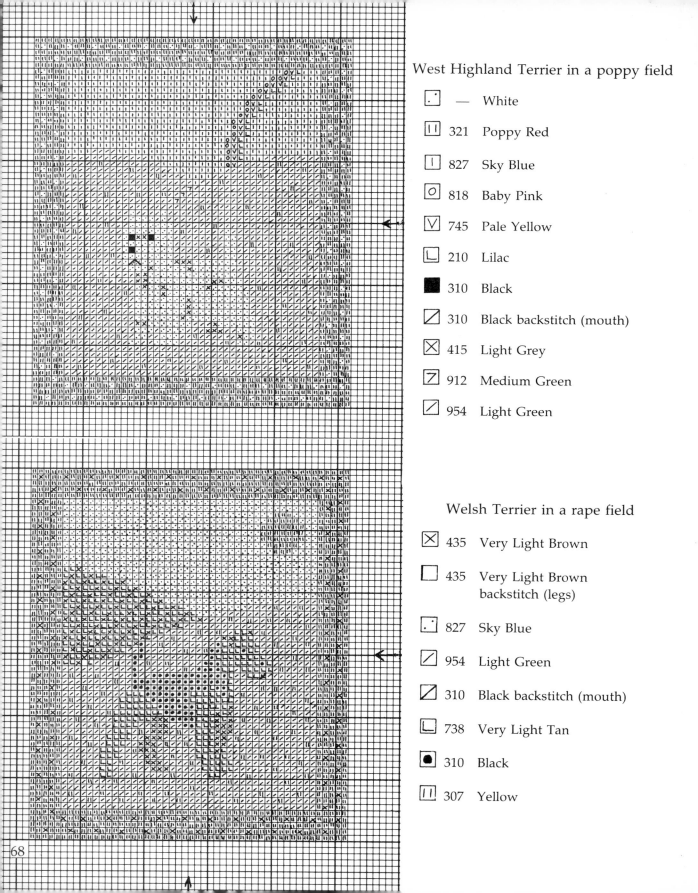

West Highland Terrier in a poppy field

⊡	—	White
Ⅱ	321	Poppy Red
Ⅰ	827	Sky Blue
O	818	Baby Pink
V	745	Pale Yellow
L	210	Lilac
■	310	Black
╱	310	Black backstitch (mouth)
⊠	415	Light Grey
7	912	Medium Green
╱	954	Light Green

Welsh Terrier in a rape field

⊠	435	Very Light Brown
☐	435	Very Light Brown backstitch (legs)
⊡	827	Sky Blue
╱	954	Light Green
╱	310	Black backstitch (mouth)
L	738	Very Light Tan
●	310	Black
Ⅱ	307	Yellow

Dachshund in a bluebell field

⊘	954	Light Green
⊡	433	Medium Brown
⊟	827	Sky Blue
⊙	310	Black
▢	318	Medium Grey backstitch (eye)
⊙	318	Medium Grey
⊠	437	Light Tan
⫴	799	Medium Blue
⌴	—	White
▢	304	Red backstitch (windows)
⊟	304	Red

Corgi in an orchard

⊟	827	Sky Blue
⊟	433	Medium Brown
⊘	954	Light Green
⊡	437	Light Tan
■	310	Black
⊙	—	White
⊠	435	Very Light Brown
⊏	415	Light Grey
⫴	321	Poppy Red
⌴	701	Green

Any colour can be used.

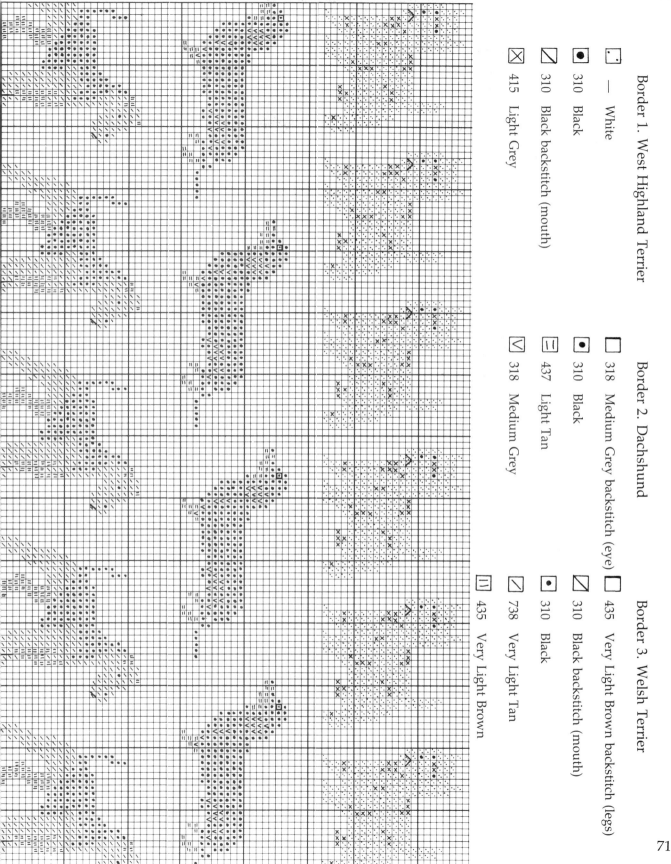

Border 1. West Highland Terrier

- `⠒` White
- `—` 310 Black
- `⟋` 310 Black backstitch (mouth)
- `☒` 415 Light Grey

Border 2. Dachshund

- `☐` 318 Medium Grey backstitch (eye)
- `●` 310 Black
- `〓` 437 Light Tan
- `∨` 318 Medium Grey

Border 3. Welsh Terrier

- `☐` 435 Very Light Brown backstitch (legs)
- `⟍` 310 Black backstitch (mouth)
- `●` 310 Black
- `⟋` 738 Very Light Tan
- `‖` 435 Very Light Brown

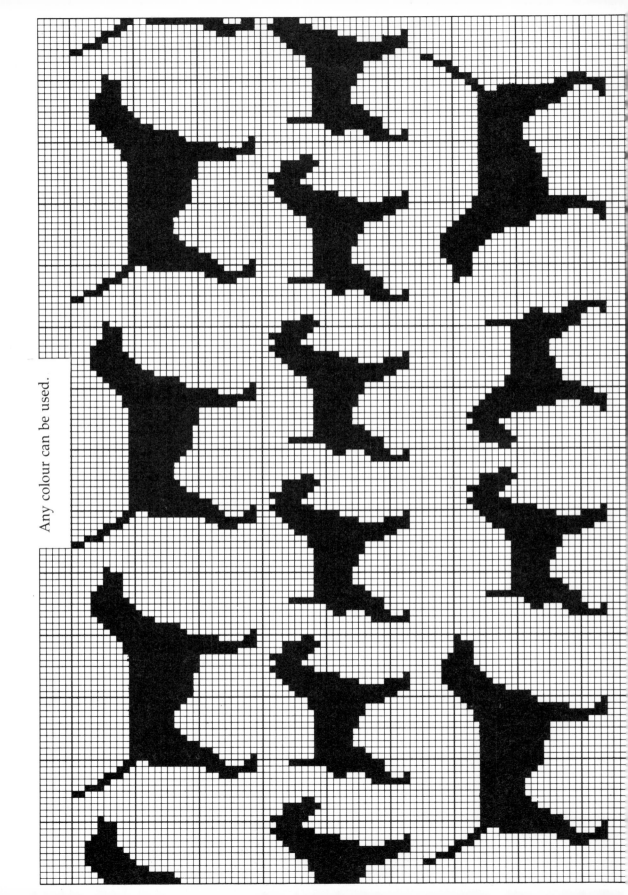

Any colour can be used.

72

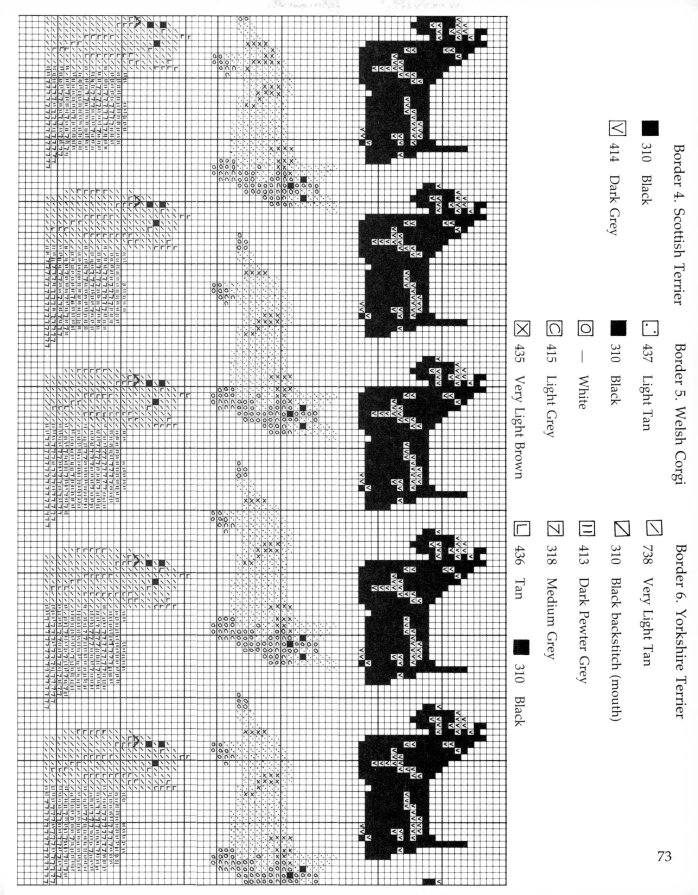

Border 4. Scottish Terrier

Symbol	No.	Colour
■	310	Black
V	414	Dark Grey

Border 5. Welsh Corgi

Symbol	No.	Colour
·	437	Light Tan
■	310	Black
O	—	White
C	415	Light Grey
X	435	Very Light Brown

Border 6. Yorkshire Terrier

Symbol	No.	Colour
/	738	Very Light Tan
/	310	Black backstitch (mouth)
II	413	Dark Pewter Grey
7	318	Medium Grey
L	436	Tan
■	310	Black

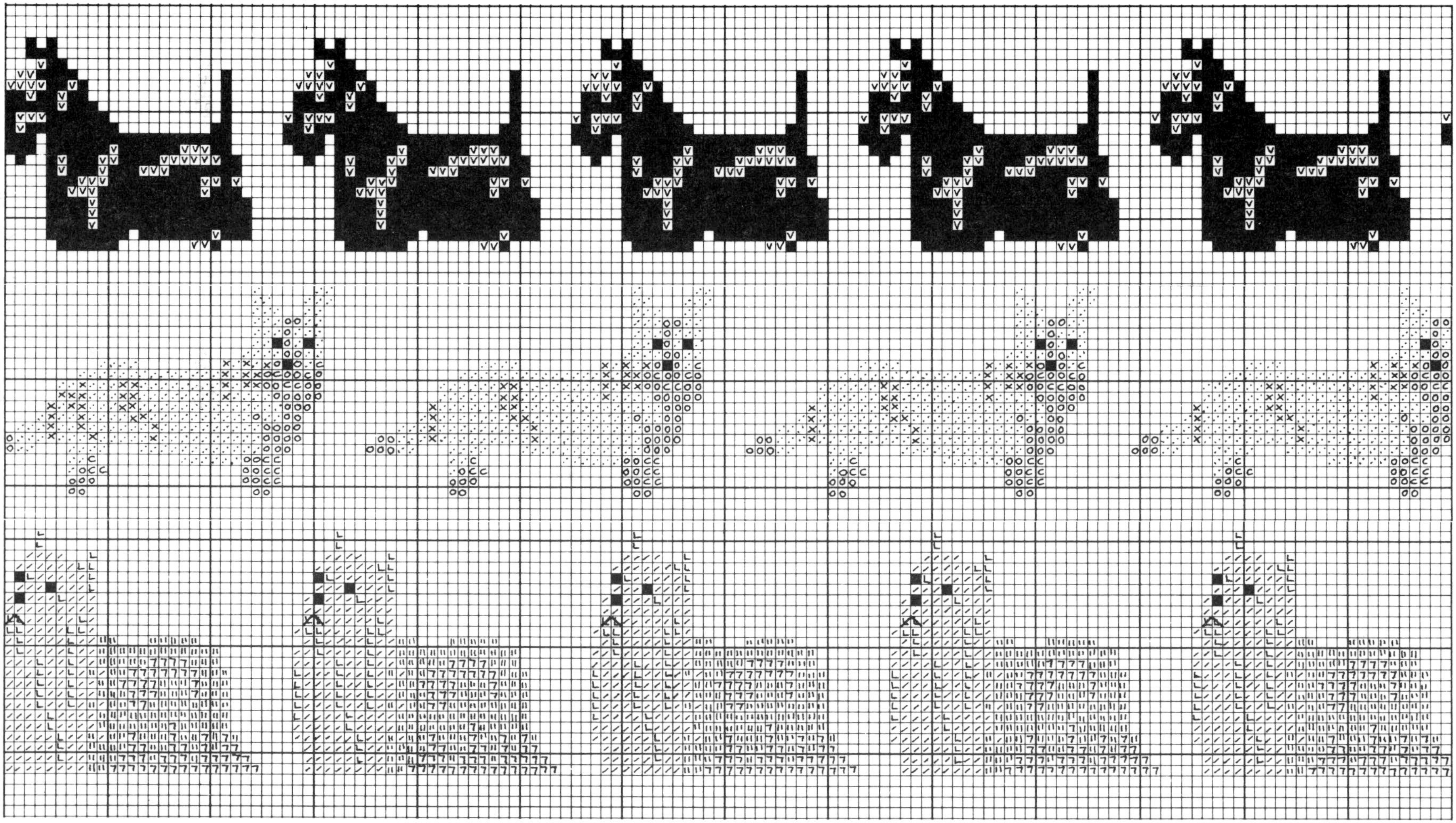

Love me, love my dog

	799	Blue		310	Black backstitch (mouth)
●	321	Poppy Red	O	415	Light Grey
✕	554	Lilac	◢	310	Black
∴	—	White			

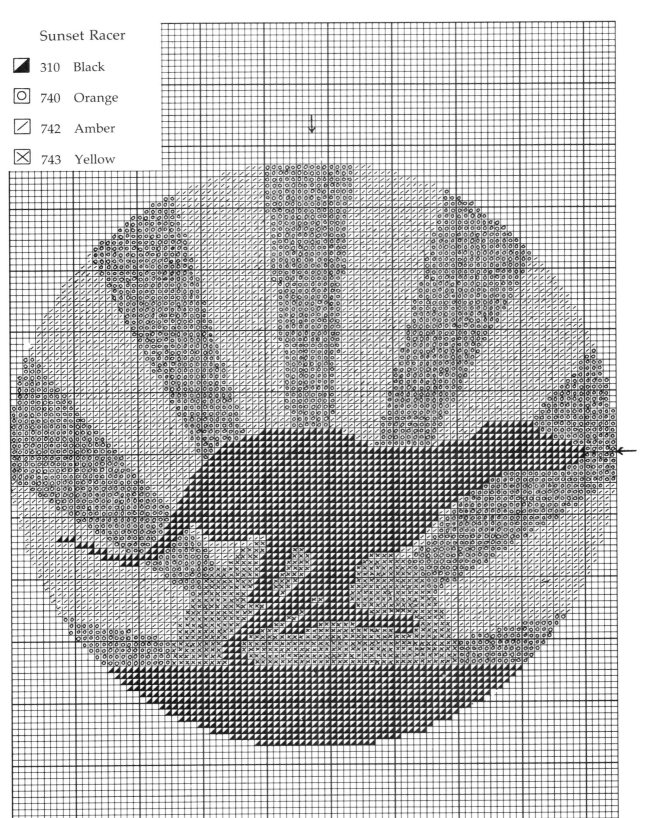

Sunset Racer

	310	Black
	740	Orange
	742	Amber
	743	Yellow

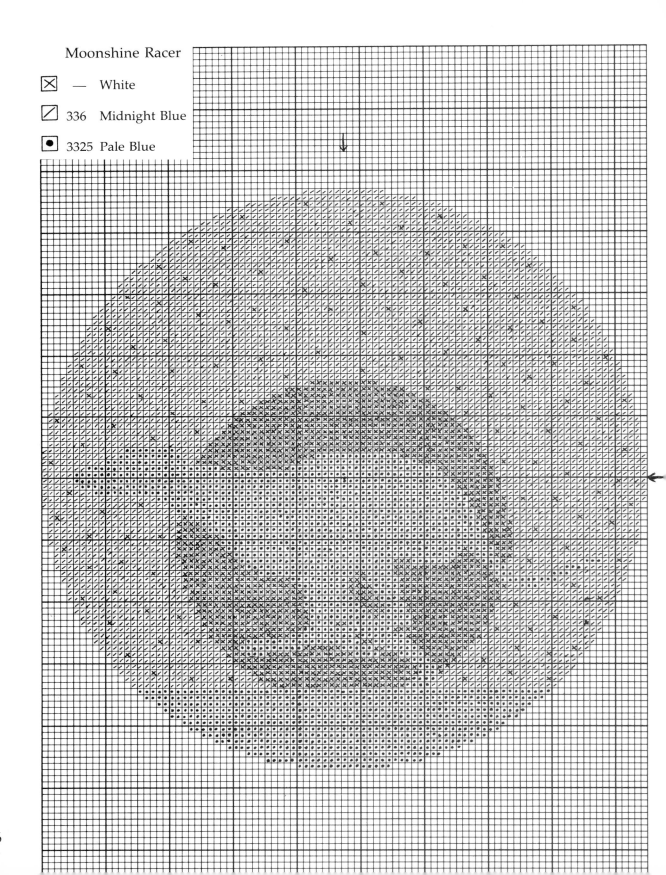

Moonshine Racer

☒	—	White
◪	336	Midnight Blue
⬤	3325	Pale Blue

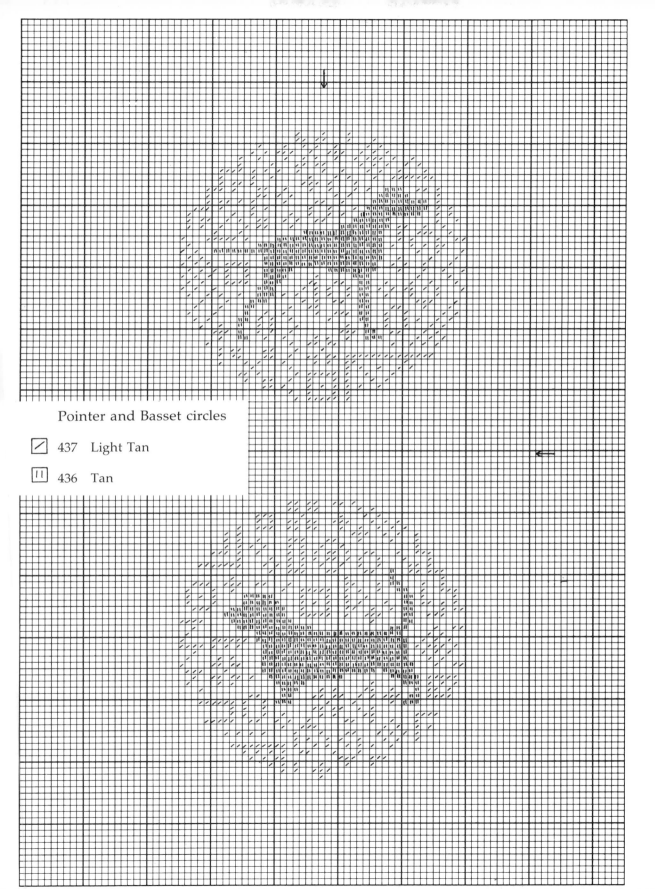

Pointer and Basset circles

| ⟋ | 437 | Light Tan |
| ‖ | 436 | Tan |

Great Dane panel

● 321 Poppy Red

Index of breeds

Basenji 19
Basset Hound   20, 70, 77
Beagle   21, 22, 72
Bernese Mountain Dog   23
Border Collie   24
Borzoi   25
Boston Terrier   26
Braque Saint Germain   27
Bull Terrier   28
Cavalier King Charles Spaniel   29
Chihuahua   30
Chow-Chow   31
Dachshund   32, 33, 69, 71
Dalmatian   34, 35
Doberman   36
English Setter   37
Eurasier   38
German Shepherd   39, 40
Golden Cocker Spaniel   41
Golden Retriever   42
Great Dane   43, 78
Greyhound   44, 45, 46, 75, 76

Jack Russell   47
Maltese   48
Pointer   70, 77
Poodle   49
Rottweiler   50
Rough Collie   51
Saluki   52
Samoyed   53
Scottish Terrier   73
Siberian Husky   54
Springer Spaniel   55
Staffordshire Bull Terrier   56
St Bernard   57
Toy Fox Terrier   58
Toy Spitz   59
Weimaraner   60
Welsh Corgi   61, 69, 73
Welsh Terrier   68, 71
West Highland Terrier   68, 71, 74
Wire Fox Terrier   62, 72
Yellow Labrador   63, 64
Yorkshire Terrier   65, 73